Gordon Ramsay
Chef for all seasons

with Roz Denny

photographs by Georgia Glynn Smith

Quadrille

For my three little stars - Megan, Jack and Holly.

May you all grow up to love food as much as I do.

Page 2: Salade tiède of mousserons,
mussels and crosnes (recipe on page 128)

Publishing Director: Anne Furniss
Consultant Art Director: Helen Lewis
Project Editor: Norma MacMillan
Design Assistant: Jim Smith
Editorial Assistant: Helen Desmond
Production: Julie Hadingham

This edition first published in 2010 by
Quadrille Publishing Limited,
Alhambra House,
27-31 Charing Cross Road,
London WC2H 0LS

ISBN: 978 184400 876 6

Printed and bound in China

contents

Introduction

When it comes to food, I am a man of many moods shaped by influences both from within my immediate circle and by what is going on outside. I am constantly on the move and rarely still. There is still so much more to discover, to taste and to try out. The success of our menus depends on a balance of popular choices and experimenting with new flavours and ideas to push the boundaries out still further. Perfection of skills and technique reassures our customers, but constant creativity keeps them coming back for more.

So when my chefs and I discuss menus late into the night after service, we must be aware of what raw ingredients are at their best for us to exploit to full advantage. Our decisions are based not just on the quality of the ingredients but also on the appropriateness for the time of year. There is no point putting a rich aromatic game stew on a summer menu, for example, when customers want a light dish, even if we could buy perfect game 'out of season' from the other side of the world.

Modern air refrigerator transport has meant seasonal boundaries have become blurred. But these are novelties I am not interested in. I won't use out-of-season foods from another hemisphere unless they are as good as our own home-grown produce in season. Some foods defy all odds to be cultivated in another time zone and their scarcity makes me that much more appreciative when they do take centre stage in my kitchen. They say a good chef is as good as the brigade behind him (yes, yes to that), but good suppliers and producers are where it begins, and I am constantly grateful to mine who share my passion and enthusiasm for good food.

This book is a collection of recipes using foods not only at their best in the seasons, but also dishes that suit the seasons, with ingredients that can be found most of the year round. You should find most of the recipes quite simple to prepare and cook because foods used in the peak of seasonal supply and perfection are best cooked simply. Each season begins with personal reflections on foods I most associate with the time of year. In addition, I pass on to you ideas of combinations of flavours, colours and textures that have worked so well for me. Some choices you may find surprising, but I hope their inclusion will encourage you to try them out.

Chelsea, London.

spring

Spring starts in my kitchen around March. The cold winds may still blow outside, but our spirits are lifted when the suppliers start to bring in treats from the warmer South of France. The lengthening of the days and the anticipation of the best of new season's produce perk us all up in the restaurant kitchen.

One of the first foods to appear are sweet **peas** in pods. They are so tender that you can just pop the pods and scoop out the tiny peas to eat raw. In France housewives like to cook the peas still in their pods because the pods are tender and full of flavour. I have a particular fondness for peas as they were the first vegetable I was allowed to prepare in a Paris kitchen, when I was promoted from sorbets onto 'veg' prep station. I had truly arrived! Peas are great with fish – I use the bigger ones puréed in a fish velouté. I am not wild about peas served cold, although I remember once enjoying a pea vinaigrette with cold lobster in Paris.

In the days of nouvelle cuisine many British chefs were accused of using baby **carrots** (and other baby veg) only as a garnish. The criticism haunted many of them, but now young carrots are back in favour, no longer on the back burner of fashion. Available for a good six months of the year, baby carrots first appear in spring, and we are able to get excellent locally grown carrots, straight and full of flavour. We just scrape and cook them lightly in butter with a splash of water. They're terrific with spring lamb, of course, but also try them with a braised fillet of cod, or cut them into thin julienne strips and serve them as a vegetable 'spaghetti'. Another idea is to cook them briefly and then souse in vinaigrette to serve cool.

To my mind, the Rolls Royce of spring vegetables are baby *fèves*, or **broad beans**. In France they are used as a luxurious garnish, or cooked in the same way as new peas – in the pods for a soup. My days at Jamin, Joël Robuchon's restaurant in Paris, saw me spending hours preparing *fèves* for the light, fantastic 'cappuccino' of *fèves* with baby lobster, one of the favourite spring starters on his menu. I've also eaten them as a warm salad with grilled cuttlefish. *Fèves* have a lovely earthy taste, and are good in many country-style dishes, such as with potato gnocchi or a salad with ricotta. Peas and *fèves* together make a good plateful, complementing each other in every way. Whilst one is sweet and tender, the other is fuller and more 'meaty' in texture. They work nicely as a twosome.

In top kitchens, **baby leaf spinach** enjoys a designer-label status, but many trainee chefs make the mistake of boiling and squeezing the life out of the young delicate leaves. If my young commis want to please me, they just check for bruised leaves and stray weeds. When it comes to baby leaf spinach there are lots of don'ts: don't pinch off the stalks, don't wash roughly, don't crush in a spinner, don't boil smothered in water and, please, don't

ever squeeze or chop the wilted leaves. The best of the best baby leaf spinach comes to us in the spring. We dress it simply in vinaigrette or cook it just with a tablespoon of water and a knob of butter. Sometimes it is so delicate that we simply put a small mound of fresh leaves straight onto a piping hot plate. They wilt instantly and that's all the cooking needed.

Another vegetable that features quite regularly in my cooking is **pak choi**, which is a pretty Chinese cabbage with stems that look like Swiss chard and a flavour that is a glorious blend of spinach and artichokes. Our supplies come in at the end of spring and last well into midsummer. We cook the baby-size ones whole, allowing one per portion. They make a great presentation vegetable with roasted poussins, grilled John Dory or poached salmon. Pak choi is also ideal for stir-frying, as it cooks in seconds in a hot wok.

If *fèves* are the Rolls Royce of spring ingredients, then I'd describe **white asparagus** as a Ferrari on a test drive because it disappears so fast. Even white truffles have a longer season. I get really excited when it comes into the kitchens. The pearly-white cigar shapes have a gentle delicate flavour, much kinder on the palate than the more robust green asparagus. The stalks need just a little peeling. We always serve white asparagus as whole spears, often simply dressed in vinaigrette. The Americans are mad for it, and the French adore it with chicken (*poulet de Bresse*, of course) and some sautéed morels.

In season for much longer than white, **green asparagus** is particularly good as a garnish for main dishes. The stalks are often woodier than white

spears, because they have a lower water content, so we peel almost the whole length, to nearer the tips. Our usual preparation is to blanch and refresh them, and then reheat in a little buttery water just before serving.

Two other varieties are the rare, pencil-thin wild asparagus and the stunningly pretty water asparagus, which is a delicate spring green with tips like baby sheaves of wheat. It's wonderful with fish dishes.

Root and tuber vegetables have a special place in our culinary repertoire. Up amongst the most favoured are **Jerusalem artichokes**, which, although available year round, we particularly enjoy using in early spring. Despite the name, they are not botanically related to globe artichokes, and they have nothing to do with the Holy city. It seems that the name is somehow derived from the Italian for sunflower (*girasole*), which is what they were called when they were introduced to Europe from North America. Both Jerusalem and globe artichokes were popularised in Europe by the French, who still use them in many different ways. Jerusalem artichokes need very little peeling (which is a good thing as they are knobbly, like a juicy root of fresh ginger) and have a rich velvety texture when cooked. We take advantage of this and use them to make sublimely smooth soups. Blanched and then sautéed in a little butter, the roots colour up beautifully.

Spring marks the arrival of, for me at any rate, the ultimate mushroom – the **morel**. I must have expensive tastes because my favourite ingredients (white truffles, white asparagus and morels) all have a very short season and resist fruitful cultivation, no matter how hard clever gardeners try. Fresh morels are around for just four to six weeks. They have the strangest shape and look like spongy, brown woolly hats. Morels are quite tricky to clean and need light scrubbing (like white truffles) and quick rinsing. We stuff the larger ones with a chicken mousse and use the smaller ones in sauces. Needless to say, I do enjoy eating them with spears of white asparagus, simply dressed with vinaigrette or melted butter.

During March and April, my supplier arrives back from Italy with lovely new season's **garlic**, which he gets from the mountains in the north. Not to be confused with wild garlic, these have smaller heads than normal garlic and taste sweeter. But they still have an overpowering pungency, which can kill other flavours in a dish. You can tame this by blanching the cloves several times in boiling water. The leaves of new season's garlic, which look a little like mint leaves, can be shredded to serve in risottos, or in dishes of beef, lamb or robust fish such as halibut. I like to confit garlic cloves, unpeeled, in goose fat, then fry them until the skins become nice and crispy.

We use a lot of **parsley**, both curly and flat-leaf. Curly-leaf has a very pronounced flavour, which is mellowed by blanching in boiling water. This intensifies the glorious dark green colour too. Once the blanched parsley is refreshed in iced water, we squeeze it dry and then purée. This parsley purée is mixed into creamy potato, whisked into sauces for fish and oysters, and even used as a light thickener. Flat-leaf parsley is ideal for garnishing, as it has a pleasant cleansing effect on the palate. It should not be chopped too fine as it bruises easily.

Recently we have started serving it with sardines tossed in vinaigrette, and we also deep-fry sprigs for a fish garnish.

Chefs are sometimes accused of popularising cod so much that stocks are threatened by demand. Well, whilst I love cooking cod, I also enjoy other white fish. One is **whiting** (it's my Mum's favourite, popular in Scotland). Flaky and full of flavour, it has the strength of cod with a slightly softer flesh, making it brilliant for a brandade. Whiting is at its best in spring and quite easy to buy. Although the flesh is quite soft, it is not at all watery. I'd better say no more or whiting too will become popular and the price will start to creep up.

Have you noticed that **spring chickens** have become poussins? I suspect it has something to do with EU legislation, and that the name has been changed because they are available all year round. (The same thing has happened to spring onions, which are now called 'salad' onions.) For me, baby-size chickens will always be just right for light spring menus, so I'll stick to the original name. Supplies of spring chickens almost disappeared about ten years ago, but now they are fairly easy to get. We find people prefer to eat them at lunchtime, but not dinner, possibly because they seem lighter. My favoured cooking method is what the French called poché-grillé – we poach the birds whole in broth to par-cook them, then remove the breasts and legs and pan-roast them. That way the meat remains succulent and the flavour is enhanced by browning in a hot pan.

When it comes to meat cookery, spring is the season for new **lamb**. Somehow, heavier meats such as beef, game and, to a certain extent, pork seem

not quite appropriate for this time of year, while lamb appeals. It is tender, sweet and delicate in flavour, and the outside cooks in next to no time to a wonderful rich, caramelised, almost barbecue flavour. To my mind, almost all the best lamb is British. Our supplies come from a number of areas, depending on the season. I prefer Scottish and Welsh lamb in spring and, when possible, use milk-fed lamb. During the autumn, I like to get in lamb from the Pyrenees, where it is reared almost completely wild; later on in the season it takes on a more gamey flavour, like wild boar. Lamb is the most versatile of all meats. We use the little legs, cannons from the saddle (especially popular with our lady customers) and neck cutlets, and also the shanks for braising.

I have to confess, I'm a **Granny Smith** man because it is such a well-balanced apple – sweet and sharp with a firm juicy texture – and it is as good raw as cooked. We use it for many desserts – in iced parfaits, in fruit salads and as a sweet jus for our hallmark dessert, crème brûlée, by crushing the apple flesh at the last moment to make a simple sauce. And that's not all. Sliced wafer thin, dipped in stock syrup and then dried overnight, Granny Smiths make excellent (fat-free) tuile biscuits. You can't get a more versatile ingredient!

In late spring, small fragrant **apricots** with blushed pink skins begin to feature on our supplier's list. The apricots come from France and Spain, two countries that offer a number of wonderful recipes for this amazingly versatile fruit. We use it in both savoury dishes and in desserts. In my early days at the Aubergine, we had a pork dish with

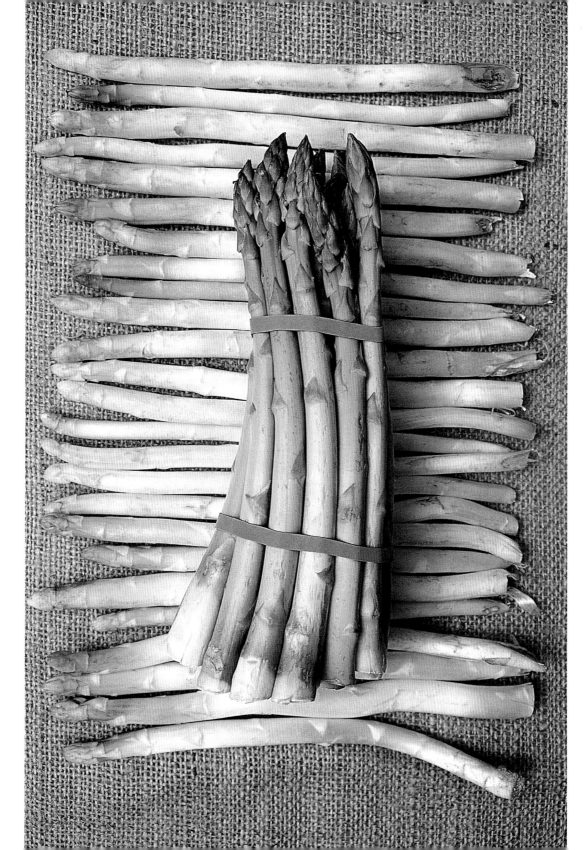

stuffed apricots on the menu, which won many fans. Clafoutis with baby apricots is a light easy pudding, or the fruits can be poached in a little cinnamon- and anise-scented syrup to serve with creamy rice pudding. The supply of small apricots lasts until the start of summer, when larger fruits arrive. These we make into a chutney to serve with foie gras (like the Peach Chutney on page 213). Out of season, we use half-dried French apricots (what the French call *mi-cuit*) that need no pre-soaking. They are brilliant for jams.

The exotic fragrance of **mangoes** is simply wonderful. When buying, don't choose a mango that is too ripe – you need an edge of sharpness to balance the luscious sweetness. For savoury cooking, buy fruits that are hard and slightly acidic. Match them with sweet seafood or with chargrilled chicken or pork and a hint of aromatic curry spices. Underripe mangoes also make good relishes and chutneys. In the dessert menu, mangoes go well with butterscotch flavours, but my ultimate favourite 'marriage' has to be with coffee and cream, which we use in a sweet ravioli recipe. For this, peel a large, firm mango and cut wafer-thin slices. Soak them in stock syrup for a couple of hours to soften, then drain and pat dry. Make a filling from seriously strong espresso coffee, thick crème fraîche and softly whipped double cream, sweetening slightly. Scoop this into balls and lay between the sheets of softened mango.

I could wax lyrical about **rhubarb**. In spring we get tender, day-glo pink stalks, which are sometimes called 'forced' rhubarb because they are grown in hothouses or covered with tall pots (this makes them grow straight and tall). Champagne rhubarb is the most

tender and sweet. We can generally get rhubarb all year round, from either Kent or Holland, so when one supply is out, the other is in. Until the late 1940s this plant was classified as a vegetable, but it is now called a fruit. I use it as both. As a vegetable, we fry it and mix with choucroute, or use it to make a fantastic sauce for fish and lobster (this is quite a talking point at any dinner party) –

sauté the chopped rhubarb in a little butter with salt and sugar, simmer gently in Vegetable Nage (page 212) to a purée, then mix with some vinaigrette. Another savoury idea is to sauté rhubarb in butter, then deglaze with grenadine syrup and serve as a quick relish for foie gras or pan-fried liver. For me, the nicest sweet way to cook rhubarb is roasted with sugar, butter and vanilla, to serve with crème brûlée.

Spring pea soup

This is a light creamy soup that has everything going for it – a tempting colour, velvety-smooth texture and a wonderful fresh flavour. Pea and bacon are a popular combination. I like to use bacon from Alsace, but another lightly smoked, dry-cure streaky bacon would be equally perfect.

SERVES 4 AS A STARTER

100g lightly smoked streaky bacon
   (preferably Alsace Ventrech), rind removed
2 shallots, sliced
2 tablespoons olive oil
400g fresh peas in pods, podded
2 tablespoons dry white wine
1 litre Light Chicken Stock (page 212)
   or Vegetable Nage (page 212)
100ml double cream, plus a little extra to serve
sea salt and freshly ground black pepper

1 Reserve 4 rashers of bacon and chop the rest. Place the chopped bacon in a saucepan with the shallots and oil. Heat until sizzling, then sweat over a low heat for about 5 minutes.
2 Add the peas and cook for a further 2–3 minutes. Pour in the wine and cook until it has evaporated.
3 Stir in the stock or nage and 250ml of water, and bring to the boil. Season, and simmer for 15 minutes. Whiz in a food processor or blender until smooth, then pass through a fine sieve into a bowl, rubbing with the back of a ladle. Leave to cool and then refrigerate.
4 Meanwhile, grill the reserved bacon rashers until crispy. (In the restaurant we bake the rashers between two heavy baking sheets to keep them straight and flat, but you may prefer the crinkly look.) Drain well on kitchen paper towel so they aren't greasy. Keep warm.
5 When the soup is well chilled, check the seasoning and whisk in the cream. Season again. Serve in bowls with a little extra cream trickled on top and a floating bacon rasher.

Jerusalem artichoke soup with morels

Once regarded as a boring winter vegetable, Jerusalem artichokes are now enjoying a revival and are back in fashion. At New York's Daniel's Restaurant, they just scrub the roots rather than peeling them. You can do that for this soup, which will give it a rustic pale grey-beige colour. If peeled, the soup will be paler.

Fresh morels have a very short season, so you should try to make the most of them when they're available. We always prepare them a good hour before cooking, washing them very carefully – ours are grown in sand, and even a few grains can ruin this sublimely smooth soup – and then leaving them to dry. Out of season, you can use 50g dried morels, first rehydrating them in warm water. **SERVES 4 AS A STARTER**

150g small fresh morels
400g fresh Jerusalem artichokes
juice of 1 small lemon
3 tablespoons olive oil
2 shallots, chopped
100ml dry white wine

1 litre Light Chicken Stock (page 212)
 or Vegetable Nage (page 212)
150ml double cream
25g butter
a little freshly grated nutmeg
sea salt and freshly ground black pepper

1 Cut the morels in half lengthways, then rinse well in cold running water to extract all the sand. Pat dry on kitchen paper towel and leave for 1 hour to dry completely.

2 Either scrub the artichokes or peel thinly with a swivel peeler. Fill a bowl with cold water and add the lemon juice. Cut each artichoke into slices and drop immediately into the acidulated water (this will stop them browning). Leave to soak for 5 minutes, then drain and pat dry.

3 Heat 2 tablespoons of the oil in a large saucepan and gently sauté the shallots for 5 minutes. Add the artichoke slices and cook for another 5 minutes.

4 Add the wine and cook until it has all evaporated. Pour in the stock or nage. Bring to the boil, season and simmer for 15 minutes or until the artichoke slices are softened.

5 Whiz in a food processor or blender, then pass through a sieve, rubbing with the back of a ladle. Return to the pan and mix in the cream. (At this point, you could chill and freeze the soup to serve later.) Heat until on the point of boiling, then set aside.

6 Heat the remaining oil with the butter in a frying pan and sauté the morels for about 5 minutes, stirring often. Season and sprinkle with a little freshly grated nutmeg. Drain on kitchen paper towel.

7 Reheat the soup, if necessary. Ladle into four warmed soup plates and scatter over the morels. Serve quickly. No garnish needed, save the morels – simple and sublime!

Asparagus soup
with fresh cheese croûtes

The lightest of spring soups, this has dainty floats of chèvre and mascarpone croûtes made from a ficelle (thin baguette). The soup can be made ahead and then reheated to serve.
SERVES 4 AS A STARTER

500g fresh green asparagus
2 tablespoons olive oil
1 medium onion, finely chopped
1 small carrot, finely chopped
20g butter
2 sprigs fresh thyme
1 litre Light Chicken Stock (page 212)
  or Vegetable Nage (page 212)
sea salt and freshly ground black pepper

To serve
1 ficelle (thin baguette)
2 cloves garlic, peeled
some light olive oil, for shallow frying
100g semi-soft chèvre, rind removed
1 tablespoon mascarpone

1 Trim the base of the asparagus spears, and use a swivel peeler to peel the skin from the stalks if a little tough. Cut off 12 tips about 5cm long. Chop the rest of the asparagus.

2 Heat the oil in a large saucepan and gently sauté the onion and carrot for about 5 minutes. Add the butter and, when melted, stir in the chopped asparagus and thyme. Sauté for 5 minutes, then cover and sweat over a low heat for a further 15 minutes until the asparagus is nicely softened, stirring occasionally.

3 Pour in the stock and add some seasoning. Bring to the boil, then cover and simmer for just 5 minutes – this keeps the flavour fresh. Check the texture of the asparagus stalks – they should be very tender. Remove the thyme sprig.

4 Lift the vegetables into a food processor or blender using a slotted spoon, reserving the liquid in the pan. Whiz until creamy, slowly adding the liquid to the processor bowl. For a velvety texture, pass the purée through a sieve back into the saucepan, rubbing with the back of a ladle. Check the seasoning and set aside.

5 Blanch the reserved asparagus tips in boiling water for 2 minutes, then drain and plunge into a bowl of iced water. Drain again and set aside.

6 To make the pretty croûtes, cut the ficelle into 1cm slices. Allow 2–3 slices per head. (You may not need all the bread.) Rub the slices on both sides with the garlic. Heat a thin layer of oil in a frying pan and, when hot, cook until golden brown and crisp on both sides. Drain immediately on kitchen paper towel and cool.

7 Beat the chèvre with the mascarpone and season lightly. Spread in attractive swirls on the croûtes.

8 Reheat the soup, check the seasoning and pour into warmed soup bowls. Float the croûtes and asparagus tips on top and serve.

Spinach velouté soup
with goat's cheese quenelles

Velvety-smooth, vibrant green and very simple – just the pure flavour of the vegetables topped with a light and silky cloud of goat's cheese and mascarpone. **SERVES 4 AS A STARTER**

400g fresh leaf spinach
2 tablespoons olive oil
1 medium potato, about 200g,
   peeled and thinly sliced
a little freshly grated nutmeg
100g fresh soft goat's cheese
40g mascarpone
1 tablespoon chopped fresh chives
150ml double cream
sea salt and freshly ground black pepper

1 Pick over the spinach, discarding any large, tough stalks and bruised leaves. Wash the remainder well in two changes of cold water, then shake off the excess water.

2 Heat the oil in a large saucepan and sauté the potato for about 5 minutes until soft. Add the spinach and stir it over the heat until well wilted.

3 Add 1 litre of water plus seasoning to taste and a little grated nutmeg. Bring to the boil, stirring. Partly cover the pan and simmer for about 15 minutes, stirring once or twice.

4 Meanwhile, beat the goat's cheese and mascarpone together until softly stiff, and fold in the chives. Season if you want to. I don't. Set aside.

5 Ladle the soup into a food processor or blender and whiz until smooth. Pass through a sieve back into the saucepan, rubbing with the back of a ladle.

6 Stir in the cream and slowly bring to the boil. Adjust the seasoning. Simmer for a minute or two.

7 Ladle the soup into warmed bowls. Shape the goat's cheese mixture into quenelles, or just carefully drop spoonfuls in the centre of the soup, and serve immediately.

Variation
For a special occasion, I sometimes make this soup with oysters. I shuck eight, saving all the juices. The four largest oysters I poach gently in the juices for a minute or two, then drain, reserving the juices. The other four I whiz in the food processor with the spinach and potato mixture. All saved oyster juices are added at this point. When the soup is served, I place a poached oyster in the centre of each bowl and spoon the goat's cheese mix on top.

Pillows of ricotta gnocchi with peas and fèves

If you have the impression that gnocchi is doughy and boring, then let me persuade you to try making potato gnocchi. They are much lighter than semolina gnocchi. Anyone who enjoys pottering about the kitchen and cooking should have a grand time with these!

SERVES 4 AS A STARTER

1kg large waxy potatoes
(preferably Desirée or Maris Piper)
175g plain flour, plus extra for shaping
1 tablespoon fine sea salt
1 teaspoon freshly ground pepper
(preferably white)
1 free-range egg, beaten

100g ricotta cheese
75g butter
200g podded fresh peas
200g podded fresh baby *fèves* (broad beans)
3 tablespoons Classic Vinaigrette (page 213)
2 tablespoons chopped fresh parsley
sea salt and freshly ground black pepper

1 Boil the potatoes still in their skins until just tender. Drain and peel them whilst hot. (We do this wearing rubber gloves to protect our hands – fondly referred to by my young commis as 'the Marigolds'). Cut each potato into quarters and spread out on a baking sheet.

2 Dry off in the oven preheated to 200°C, Gas 6 for about 5 minutes. Then mash until smooth. The best way to do this is to push the potato through a ricer. Failing that a masher will do, but not an electric beater or food processor, or the texture will become gluey.

3 Mix the potato with the flour, fine sea salt, white pepper, egg and ricotta cheese. The mixture will be like a soft dough. Don't overbeat or the gnocchi will be tough. Spread out the mixture on a plate and chill until firm.

4 Shape the potato mixture into long cigar shapes about 1.5cm thick. Using the back of a table knife, cut across into 3cm lengths. (See photographs of this technique on page 220.) Bring a large pan of water to the boil. Add the gnocchi pillows and simmer for about 5 minutes. (You may have to cook them in batches.) Drain well and plunge immediately into ice-cold water. Drain again and pat dry on kitchen paper towel.

5 Melt the butter and heat slowly until it turns a light brown colour. Strain though a fine sieve and discard the solids. Pour the butter into a frying pan and lightly fry the gnocchi until nicely coloured all over. Season and keep warm.

6 Meanwhile, cook the peas and *fèves* in lightly salted boiling water for 2–3 minutes. Drain and season. Stir in the vinaigrette to bind and then the parsley.

7 Divide the pea and *fève* salad among four plates and top with the browned gnocchi. Serve immediately.

Warm salad of ceps and white asparagus

White asparagus is popular in Europe, where it is associated with fine dining. The spears are almost always served whole. Between April and May I am able to buy plump white asparagus grown in the Vale of Evesham. It is so tender there is no need for any peeling, just a thin trimming of the stalk end. It makes a good simple salad, topped with sautéed sliced ceps and a brown butter sauce. **SERVES 4 AS A STARTER**

about 12 large spears, or 24–30 thinner
    spears, fresh white asparagus
juice of 1 lemon
4 tablespoons olive oil
75g unsalted butter
200g fresh ceps, bases trimmed, sliced
2 tablespoons fresh flat-leaf parsley leaves
sea salt and freshly ground black pepper

1 Prepare the asparagus first. Trim the ends. Bring a shallow pan of salted water to the boil and add half of the lemon juice and a tablespoon of the oil. Add the asparagus spears and blanch for about 4 minutes, then drain carefully (so as not to damage the tips) and plunge into a wide shallow bowl of iced water. Leave until cold, then drain carefully again and pat lightly dry.
2 Make the brown butter. Heat the butter gently in a small saucepan, then turn up the heat and cook until the butter just turns brown. Watch it like a hawk! Tip it quickly into a cup to stop the browning. Set aside.
3 Heat the remaining oil in a frying pan and fry the ceps, stirring and tossing, until just softened. Add the parsley leaves, season and remove to a plate.
4 Wipe out the pan and tip in the brown butter, leaving the solids behind in the cup. Heat gently, then lay in the asparagus spears. Heat carefully until hot, then sprinkle over the rest of the lemon juice.
5 Arrange 4 asparagus spears on each plate, drizzle over any pan juices and spoon over the ceps. That's it – naturally simple.

Salad of avocado and crab with pink grapefruit dressing

You cannot beat classic combinations of flavour and colour – avocado and seafood win fans every time. But instead of a creamy mayonnaise-style dressing, try mixing the seafood – here crab – with a light vinaigrette spiked with star-burst bubbles of pink grapefruit. The pastel shades and fresh flavours will make this a very popular starter.

Fresh crab meat is the best choice. If you have to use frozen, press the crab meat in a colander using the back of a ladle, to remove all excess liquid. **SERVES 4 AS A STARTER**

1 pink grapefruit
150ml Classic Vinaigrette (page 213)
2 large, just ripe avocados
2 plum tomatoes, skinned, seeded and chopped
juice of ½ lime
1 teaspoon finely chopped shallot or spring onion
few drops of hot pepper sauce (optional)
150g white crab meat
about 100g small salad leaves (a mixture, or
    mâche or small wild rocket leaves alone)
sea salt and freshly ground black pepper

1 Cut the peel and pith from the grapefruit, then using a sharp fruit knife cut between the membranes to release the segments. (Do this over a bowl to catch the juice.) Add the segments to the bowl and break into tiny 'teardrops' with the tines of a fork. Mix in 100ml of the vinaigrette and set aside.

2 Make a guacamole. Halve and stone the avocados and scoop out the flesh into a shallow bowl. Mash to a chunky purée using a fork, then mix in the tomatoes, lime juice, shallot or onion, pepper sauce to taste (if using) and seasoning.

3 Carefully check the crab meat for any bits of shell. (We do this on a flat plate with the back of a fork.) Season nicely and bind with 1 tablespoon of the remaining vinaigrette.

4 Toss the salad leaves with the last of the vinaigrette, and season too.

5 To assemble the salad, use a large plain scone cutter 7–8cm in diameter. Place the cutter in the centre of a medium plate and spoon in a quarter of the guacamole. Lightly press a quarter of the crab meat on top, then make little towering piles of salad leaves on top of that. Gently lift off the cutter. (See photographs of this technique on page 221.) Wipe the cutter inside, and repeat three more times on three more plates. (Alternatively, you can simply spoon the three salads on top of each other on the plates.)

6 Finally, dribble tiny teaspoonfuls of the grapefruit dressing around each salad and serve.

Steamed scallops and asparagus with lemon grass butter sauce

Whoever said steamed food was boring? Not me. For example, I love the pure delicate flavours of sweet scallops and pencil-thin asparagus steamed in their own juices, then gently coated in a fragrant beurre blanc. *Ask the fishmonger to open the scallops for you, and to give you the cup-shaped shells. In the restaurant we usually throw away the corals, but you can cook them if you wish. Chinese bamboo steaming baskets are cheap and easy to find if you take a trip to any major Chinatown. I use them often for fish and vegetables.* **SERVES 4 AS A STARTER**

4–6 large scallops, removed from their shells,
   with 4 of the rounded shells saved
150g thin green asparagus tips
1 tablespoon chopped fresh chervil or chives
sea salt and freshly ground black pepper

Sauce
1 stalk fresh lemon grass, tough
   outer leaves stripped off
2 shallots, finely chopped
100ml dry white wine
1 teaspoon white wine vinegar
2 tablespoons double cream
100g unsalted butter, chilled and
   cut in small cubes

1 Rinse the scallops well and pat dry. Feel for the hard nugget of flesh on the side and pull this off. Very plump scallops are best sliced horizontally in three, otherwise simply slice in half.

2 Scrub out the shells and divide the asparagus among them. Season lightly and place the scallop slices on top, adding the corals if you are using them.

3 Prepare a pan of boiling water over which your bamboo steamer will rest. While the water is heating, make the butter sauce.

4 Chop the lemon grass very finely, discarding any hard woody bits. Wrap and tie up in a piece of muslin. Cook the shallots and lemon grass in the white wine for about 5 minutes until nicely softened and the liquid has reduced right down to almost nothing. Remove the lemon grass bag. Add the vinegar and cook until evaporated, which takes seconds.

5 Stir in the cream, season and bring to a simmer. (The cream helps to stabilise the sauce.) Drop in a couple of cubes of butter and beat vigorously with a small whisk until melted and emulsified. Drop in some more butter cubes and whisk again. When all the cubes have been added, mix in 2 tablespoons of cold water and remove from the heat. Cover the top of the sauce with cling film or a butter paper and set aside to keep warm.

6 Bring the pan of water to a good head of steam. Season the scallops and place the shells in the basket base. Place over the pan and cover with the lid. Steam for 3½–4 minutes, depending on how thick the scallops are.

7 Remove the basket from the pan – take care as steam can burn badly. Lift out the shells carefully so as not to spill any juice, and put on plates, setting each shell on a small mound of rock salt. (The salt helps to keep the shells level so they don't tip over.)

8 Nappé the scallops with the butter sauce, sprinkle with the herbs and serve right away.

Whiting with a lemon and parsley crust

I think whiting is an underrated fish, eclipsed by the meatier cod and haddock. But although the flesh of whiting is more tender, the flavour is good. This recipe suits large size whiting, which your fishmonger should be able to fillet into four neat long fillets. The crust is made in an ingenious way. Instead of pressing a loose mass onto each fillet, it is pressed together as a sheet, cut and placed on top. Then the fish is cooked half submerged in liquid, with the crust poking out at the top. To complete the fresh green theme, you could serve the fish on a mound of baby leaf spinach. Just place the spinach on piping hot plates so the leaves wilt – no need to cook. **SERVES 4 AS A MAIN DISH**

1 large whiting, about 1.2kg,
  filleted in four, skin on
3 tomatoes, skinned, seeded
  and finely chopped
3 tablespoons olive oil
3 tablespoons coarsegrain mustard
1 bay leaf
2 sprigs fresh thyme
3 tablespoons double cream
sea salt and freshly ground black pepper

Crust
200g unsalted butter
200g unsweetened brioche crumbs
  or good-quality white breadcrumbs
100g curly-leaf parsley sprigs
grated zest of 2 lemons

1 Check the fillets for any pinbones, then cut each across in two to make 8 pieces. Set aside.

2 Cook the chopped tomato in 1 tablespoon of the olive oil until you have a slightly chunky purée. Season and set aside.

3 Make the crust. Blend the butter and crumbs in a food processor until crumbly. Drop in the parsley, lemon zest and seasoning, and whiz to fine crumbs. Line a wooden board with cling film and tip the buttery crumb mixture on top. Cover with more cling film, and roll out with a rolling pin to a rectangle about 1cm thick. Place this crust in the freezer to firm up for a couple of hours. Then cut into 8 pieces about the same size as the fish fillets.

4 When ready to cook, preheat the oven to 200°C, Gas 6. Spread 2 tablespoons of the mustard over the skin of the fish, then spoon on the tomato 'purée'. Finally, lift the crust cut-outs off the film and press gently on top. Lay gently in a flameproof baking dish, crust side up.

5 Put the remaining oil in a small saucepan with about 300ml of water, the herbs and seasoning. Bring to the boil. Pour the liquid down the side of the baking dish so it doesn't wet the crust. Bake, uncovered, for 8–10 minutes until the crust is light and crisp and the fish feels firm when pressed lightly in the centre. Remove from the heat and, using a long spatula, lift out the fish onto four warmed dinner plates.

6 Place the baking dish on the hob and boil down the liquid by half, then add the remaining mustard and the cream. Pour neatly around the fish. Serve with baby new potatoes.

Roast turbot with asparagus velouté

Turbot is one of the largest of the flat fish, with flesh that is both tender and quite meaty. Chefs love it because it is so accommodating and teams well with a variety of flavours. This is a lovely dish with which to welcome spring to your table, chic and yet quite casual in presentation.

SERVES 4 AS A MAIN DISH

600g fillet of turbot, skinned

250g fresh green asparagus

3 tablespoons olive oil

1 shallot, chopped

leaves from 1 sprig fresh tarragon, chopped

300ml Fish Stock (page 212)

about 50g fresh baby leaf spinach

2 tablespoons double cream

200g tagliatelle (preferably fresh)

25g butter

1 tablespoon chopped fresh chives

sea salt and freshly ground black pepper

1 Cut the fish across into four even slices and trim to neaten. Set aside.

2 Trim the bases of the asparagus spears and peel the stalks, if necessary. Chop half of the spears into small pieces; reserve the other half.

3 Heat 1 tablespoon of the oil and sauté the chopped asparagus gently with the shallot and tarragon for 5 minutes. Add half the stock and a little seasoning, and simmer, uncovered, for 3–5 minutes until tender. Add the spinach and cook until wilted.

4 Whiz the asparagus and spinach mixture in a blender or food processor until smooth. Pass through a sieve into a saucepan, rubbing with the back of a ladle. Mix in the cream and set aside until ready to serve.

5 Cook the tagliatelle in boiling salted water until just *al dente*. Drain, rinse under cold water and drain again. Return to the pan with half of the butter. Set aside. (This is what we do in the restaurant, but you may prefer to cook the pasta later, while you are cooking the fish.)

6 Cook the remaining asparagus in lightly salted boiling water for about 3 minutes until just tender. Drain, rinse under cold water, drain again and return to the pan with the remaining butter.

7 Heat the remaining oil in a large non-stick frying pan and, when hot, cook the fish for about 1 minute on each side until nicely coloured. Season the fish as it cooks. Pour in the remaining stock and bubble gently, spooning the pan juices over the fish. This part-braising keeps the fish moist. After about 3 minutes the stock should have reduced to a syrupy glaze and the fish will be just tender.

8 Heat the pasta, adding a splash of water if necessary to stop it from sticking. Season and toss in the chives. Reheat the asparagus spears.

9 Place the pasta in the centre of four warmed plates. Meanwhile, reheat the asparagus and spinach velouté. Centre the fish on top of the pasta, spoon around the hot velouté and surround with the blanched asparagus spears. Serve quickly.

Sea trout with crushed fresh peas

Wild sea trout, like salmon, can live in fresh or salt water. Slightly sweeter than salmon and a little smaller, they are at their best between April and September. Superb fish needs just the simplest of accompaniments – in this case a crushed purée of fresh summer peas bound with a little vinaigrette and enhanced with some fresh marjoram. Serve with baby new potatoes.

SERVES 4 AS A MAIN DISH

1 sea trout, about 2–2.5kg,
   filleted in two, skin on
1–2 tablespoons olive oil
500g fresh peas in pods, podded
1 tablespoon chopped fresh marjoram,
   plus marjoram leaves to garnish
2 tablespoons Classic Vinaigrette (page 213)
sea salt and freshly ground black pepper

1 Feel the fish flesh for any pinbones with your fingertips and remove them with your fingernails or tweezers. Cut each fillet across in half. Trim these 4 pieces neatly. Using the tip of a very sharp knife (or a clean craft knife), score the skin in thin parallel lines, leaving a 1cm border uncut all round. Rub both sides of the fish with the oil and set aside.

2 Cook the peas in boiling salted water for 3–4 minutes until just tender. Drain and return to the pan. Crush the peas against the side of the pan with a fork so you have a chunky purée. Season, and stir in the chopped marjoram and vinaigrette. Set aside.

3 Heat a non-stick frying pan. When you can feel a good heat rising, place the fillets in the pan, skin side down. Season and cook for about 4 minutes so the skin becomes crispy. Carefully turn and cook the other side for a minute just to brown lightly. Season again.

4 Spoon the crushed peas into the centre of four warmed dinner plates and place the fish on top. Garnish with marjoram leaves, if liked, and serve.

Spring chickens with baby pak choi in sweet-sour sauce

Oriental flavours have been enthusiastically embraced in classic European kitchens – it's all about culinary lateral thinking. I like to serve roasted poussins (aka spring chickens) with a sweet-sour sauce and tiny heads of Chinese 'spring greens' called pak choi, which are now grown commercially in European market gardens. Don't trim the pak choi – they are cooked whole. **SERVES 4 AS A MAIN DISH**

4 tablespoons olive oil
4 poussins, 500–600g each
75g butter, melted
8 heads small pak choi
2 tablespoons dark soy sauce
sea salt and freshly ground black pepper

Sauce
1 red pepper, chopped
1 yellow pepper, chopped
1 tablespoon olive oil
1 tablespoon white wine vinegar
1 teaspoon caster sugar
3 tablespoons Classic Vinaigrette (page 213)

1 First, make the sauce. Sauté the chopped peppers in the oil for about 5 minutes until softened. Deglaze with the vinegar and add the sugar, stirring until dissolved. Whiz to a fine purée in a blender or food processor with the vinaigrette. Rub through a sieve with the back of a ladle. Season and set aside.

2 Preheat the oven to 200°C, Gas 6.

3 Heat 2 tablespoons of the oil in a large frying pan. When hot, add the birds, two at a time, and brown all over. (In the restaurant we press the poussins down with our hands so they colour evenly, but this is only for the brave – or foolhardy!)

4 Place the birds in a roasting tin, open out their legs and trickle over the melted butter, pouring it through a small sieve. Season. Roast for 15–20 minutes, basting the birds at least twice – spoon up the pan juices and trickle them through the sieve again. This gives the poussins an evenly golden, crisp skin. Spoon the juices inside the birds as well if possible, for flavour. When cooked, remove from the oven and set aside to rest.

5 You can serve the birds whole, or you can serve them like this: using a very sharp knife, remove the breasts from the bone in one piece. Cut through the thigh joint and remove the legs. We then loosen and pull out the thigh bone, leaving the drumstick, but you may find this just too much trouble! Discard the carcasses. Keep the meat warm.

6 Trim the pak choi neatly and sauté whole in the remaining oil for about 3 minutes. Deglaze with the soy sauce and season with pepper only.

7 To serve, place the pak choi in the centre of four warmed plates and sit the chicken on top. Reheat the sauce gently and spoon over the chicken. This is nice with butter-dressed tagliatelle.

Grilled chicken with tagliatelle and morel velouté

This is a rustic dish par excellence – wonderful to come home to, or to make for a relaxed dinner party. I suggest chicken breasts (preferably from free-range corn-fed birds), but you could substitute guinea fowl or pheasant breasts. Try to use fresh tagliatelle from a reputable Italian deli. If that is not possible then buy a good-quality dried pasta such as De Cecco or Delverde rather than a supermarket own brand. Italians take their pasta qualities seriously, and so should we. **SERVES 4 AS A MAIN DISH**

about 100g fresh morels
3–4 tablespoons olive oil
1 large shallot, finely chopped
150ml dry white wine
500ml Dark Chicken Stock (page 212)
250ml double cream
500g tagliatelle (preferably fresh)
4 boneless chicken breasts, skin on, about 120g each
sea salt and freshly ground black pepper

1 Cut the morels in half lengthways, then rinse well in cold running water to extract all the sand. Pat dry on kitchen paper towel and leave for 1 hour to dry completely.

2 Trim half of the morels into neat shapes. Chop the rest, with the trimmings, quite finely.

3 Make the sauce ahead, if liked. Heat 1 tablespoon of the oil and gently sauté the shallot until nicely coloured, about 5 minutes. Add the finely chopped morels and continue cooking for 3 minutes. Pour in the wine and cook until reduced by half. Add the stock and season lightly. Boil until reduced by half again, then stir in the cream and simmer for 5 minutes. Pass through a sieve into a clean pan, rubbing with the back of a ladle. Check the seasoning and set aside until ready to serve.

4 Preheat the grill until hot. Brush the chicken skin lightly with a little oil and season. Grill, skin side up, for a few minutes, then lower the heat to medium and continue grilling until the skin becomes nice and crispy. Turn over and cook the other side for a couple of minutes (most of the cooking should be on the skin side). The breasts should be just firm, but not tough.

5 While the chicken is cooking, sauté the trimmed morels in 1 tablespoon of the oil for a few minutes. Make sure they are well roasted or you won't get the best flavour from them. Remove and drain on kitchen paper towel.

6 Cook the pasta in boiling salted water for 3–5 minutes if fresh, or according to pack instructions if dried. Drain, then mix in about half of the sauce and reheat gently. Reheat the remaining sauce.

7 Divide the pasta among four warmed shallow bowls. Cut the chicken into medallions and place on the pasta. Nappé the chicken with the sauce and scatter over the sautéed morels.

Herb-crusted rack of lamb with tomato farci

Lamb is a popular dish on our restaurant menu at all times of the year, but particularly associated with spring. We like to serve lamb racks with a light herb crust, which is rolled out in a sheet and pressed onto the part-roasted meat. The bits of crust that fall off are mixed into a finely chopped ratatouille mixture and spooned high into plum tomato shells. Some baby new potatoes make the nicest accompaniment. **SERVES 4 AS A MAIN DISH**

2 racks of new season's lamb,
  about 300g each, chined
4 large plum tomatoes
2 tablespoons olive oil
1 medium courgette, finely chopped
1/2 small red pepper, finely chopped
1/2 small yellow pepper, finely chopped
1/2 small aubergine, finely chopped
sea salt and freshly ground black pepper

Crust
200g unsweetened brioche crumbs
  or rich white breadcrumbs
1 tablespoon chopped fresh basil
1 tablespoon chopped fresh chives
1 teaspoon fresh thyme leaves
50g butter, softened

1 Trim the lamb racks. Remove the chine bone and long sinew. Score the fat with the tip of a sharp knife into neat diamonds.

2 Make the herb crust. Blitz the crumbs in a food processor with the herbs and seasoning, then add the butter. Whiz until the crumbly mixture can be pinched with your fingers to a paste – what the French call a *pommade*. Line a wooden board with cling film and tip the mixture on top. Cover with more cling film, and roll out with a rolling pin to a sheet approximately the same area as the fat area of the two lamb racks. Chill the crust in the cling film.

3 To prepare the tomatoes, dip briefly in boiling water and then skin. Cut off a quarter of each at the top and chop into fine dice. Scoop out the seeds from the tomato shells and discard.

4 Heat the oil in a pan and sauté the courgette, peppers and aubergine for about 5 minutes, until just softened. Season nicely, then bind together with the tomato dice and set aside.

5 Preheat the oven to 200°C, Gas 6. Heat a heavy non-stick frying pan and, when hot, brown the fat side of each lamb rack. Turn to brown as much of the meat as possible. Remove from the heat. Stand the racks upright and allow the juices to run down in the pan.

6 Cut the herb crust into two pieces the same size as the racks and press onto the hot fat surface firmly with your fingers. The *pommade* is made with less butter than normal, so it sticks better. Mix any crust trimmings into the vegetables. Set the lamb, crust side up, in a roasting tin and roast for 10–12 minutes until the meat feels lightly springy when pressed.

7 Meanwhile, fill the tomato shells with the vegetable and *pommade* mix, piling it up high. Place the tomatoes in a baking dish with a trickle of olive oil and roast in the oven with the meat until hot and the tops crisp a little.

8 Allow the lamb to rest for 5–10 minutes before cutting each rack in half or into individual cutlets. Serve with the tomatoes, and trickle over any *jus* from the roasting tin.

Rump of new season's lamb with lentils

This is a good homely dish similar to many served up and down France. We call this cut of lamb rump, but you will know it better as chump. We serve the lamb with creamy gratin potatoes. By par-cooking potatoes in milk before finishing them in ramekins, they cook more evenly. It's a neat little trick. SERVES 4 AS A MAIN DISH

4 chumps of lamb, about 200g each

3–4 tablespoons olive oil

1 sprig fresh thyme

150g Puy lentils

1 medium carrot

½ small celeriac

1 medium leek

2 tablespoons coarsely chopped fresh parsley

4 tablespoons Classic Vinaigrette (page 213)

sea salt and freshly ground black pepper

Gratin potatoes

400g medium, slightly waxy
   potatoes, such as Maris Piper

300ml milk

300ml double cream

1 clove garlic, sliced

1 sprig fresh thyme

1 bay leaf

75g Gruyère cheese, grated

1 Remove the central bone from the chumps. Trim off fat and neaten to nice rump shapes. Place in a bowl or food bag with half of the oil and the tips from the thyme sprig. Set aside to marinate in the fridge.

2 Cook the lentils in boiling salted water for about 15 minutes. Drain and season.

3 Cut the carrot, celeriac and leek into 1cm squares. Heat the remaining oil in a saucepan and sauté the vegetables until lightly browned, 5–7 minutes (we call this a *brunoise*). Mix with the lentils and half the parsley, then bind with 2 tablespoons of the vinaigrette. Set aside.

4 For the gratin potatoes, preheat the oven to 200°C, Gas 6. Peel the potatoes and slice thinly (use a mandolin or the slicing blade of a food processor). Bring the milk and cream to the boil with some sea salt, the garlic and herbs, and simmer for a couple of minutes. Add the sliced potatoes and simmer for about 5 minutes until just tender. Drain in a colander set over a bowl to catch the creamy milk.

5 Mix the potatoes gently with two-thirds of the cheese. Layer neatly into four medium ramekins or cocotte dishes, seasoning in between the layers. Spoon a little of the saved creamy milk on top of each ramekin and sprinkle with the last of the cheese. Place the ramekins on a baking sheet and bake for 8–10 minutes until the cheese just turns a golden brown.

6 Meanwhile, heat a heavy-based non-stick frying pan until really hot. Remove the lamb rumps from the bowl or food bag, wiping off any thyme tips, and brown for 3–5 minutes on each side, seasoning lightly as they cook. The lamb should be served lightly pink – medium rare.

7 Reheat the lentils and spoon into the centre of four plates. Place the rumps on top (slice them first, if you like). Deglaze the frying pan with the last of the vinaigrette, stirring for a minute, then spoon these juices over the lamb. Sprinkle with the remaining parsley. Serve the gratin potatoes, still in their individual dishes, on the same plate. Simple and delicious!

Oven-roasted caramel bananas en papillote

This is a seriously naughty pudding, so turn the page unless you wish to be tempted. If, however, you are still reading and cannot resist, then start to look for some sheets of greaseproof paper. Allow 2 medium bananas per portion. **SERVES 4**

4 tablespoons light Muscovado sugar
50g unsalted butter
100ml double cream
2 whole cloves
8 medium bananas, just ripe and not soft
a little sifted icing sugar, to dust
4 stalks fresh lemon grass
crème fraîche, to serve

1 First, make the caramel sauce. Melt the sugar in a saucepan with just a splash of water to get it under way. When dissolved and clear, raise the heat and cook for 3–5 minutes until a light-coloured caramel is formed. Remove from the heat and immediately stir in the butter. Then mix in the cream and cloves. Set aside to infuse and cool.

2 When ready to cook, preheat the oven to 200°C, Gas 6. Get four sheets of greaseproof paper ready, each about 30 x 20cm.

3 Heat a non-stick pan until nice and hot. Cut the bananas in half lengthways and dust with icing sugar. Add to the dry hot pan and allow the sugar to caramelise on the first side before turning carefully. This should take just seconds if the pan is hot enough. (You may have to caramelise the bananas in batches, wiping out the pan each time.) As soon as the bananas are caramelised, remove immediately to the centre of the sheets of greaseproof, allowing 4 halves per serving.

4 Slash each lemon grass stalk almost to the thick end and place on top of the bananas. Remove the cloves from the caramel and spoon it over the bananas.

5 Holding the two long ends of each sheet of paper up together, fold over and down several times, leaving a bit of a gap above the banana. Scrunch the ends in twists, like a cracker. Place the parcels on a baking sheet. (In the restaurant, we cut and fold the paper into 'D' shapes and dust them with sifted icing sugar before baking. The paper takes on a fantastic dark caramel gloss.)

6 Bake for 7–10 minutes until the parcels are puffed up. Serve each one on a plate, and just slash open the top to spoon in some crème fraîche. Serve as soon as possible. (Be careful when opening the bags to eat – they will expel hot steam.)

Easy mango tarts with fromage blanc sorbet

The introduction of blow torches into kitchen equipment stores has certainly made cooking more adventurous for the home cook! She (or he) can now make wonderfully quick caramelised toppings. This is one recipe where a blow torch would come in handy. The base is puff pastry, which can now be bought ready rolled. For the very best flavour, though, I suggest you make your own. **SERVES 4**

500g home-made Puff Pastry (page 214)
  or 2 x 375g packs ready-rolled puff pastry
icing sugar, to sprinkle
4 ripe medium mangoes
2 ripe passion fruits
1 tablespoon chopped fresh mint
Fromage Blanc Sorbet (page 215), to serve

1 Roll out the puff pastry to the thickness of a £1 coin. Cut out four 12cm rounds. (You could use a saucer as a template.) Place on a flat baking sheet. Prick the pastry rounds several times and chill for 20 minutes.

2 Meanwhile, preheat the oven to 200°C, Gas 6.

3 When ready to bake, place a sheet of non-stick baking parchment on the pastry rounds and fit a heavy, flat baking sheet on top so the pastry is sandwiched in between. Bake for 10–12 minutes until dark golden brown and crisp. The baking sheet on top will keep the pastry bases flat.

4 Remove the top baking sheet. Dredge the pastry rounds fairly liberally with sifted icing sugar and return to the oven to melt and glaze. Remove and slide the rounds off onto a wire rack to cool and crisp.

5 Peel each mango thinly and cut off two thick slices vertically on either side of the flat stone. Cut across the slices into half-moon shapes. Arrange on top of the pastry rounds, piling the slices towards the centre.

6 Cut open the passion fruits and scoop out the flesh into a small sieve over a bowl. Rub through the juice and pulp. Trickle this over the mango slices.

7 Sift icing sugar on the fruits, then immediately caramelise with a blow torch. If you don't have a torch, then preheat the grill until glowing red and caramelise the sugar that way. Take care, though, as the grill could also burn the pastry edge.

8 Cool the tarts a little, then sprinkle with the chopped mint. Eat warm with scoops of fromage blanc sorbet or a bought sorbet.

Baby apricot clafoutis

This French favourite is normally associated with cherries, but I like to make smaller versions using fresh apricots. These start coming into season in late spring, or you might catch the tail end of the South African supply in February/March. We serve some almond icecream alongside the clafoutis, but it is just as delicious served simply dusted with icing sugar and topped with a trickle of cream or some crème fraîche. The batter mix is best left to rest and soften for a good 24 hours beforehand. **SERVES 4**

50g toasted flaked almonds
1 tablespoon strong (bread) flour
pinch of salt
100g caster sugar
2 large free-range eggs
3 free-range egg yolks
250ml double cream
a little softened butter, for greasing
12 ripe medium apricots
icing sugar, to dust

1 First, grind the almonds to a very fine dust in a coffee grinder or nut mill (it is hard to grind such a small amount of nuts in a food processor). Tip into a food processor and whiz with the flour and salt, then add the sugar, eggs, yolks and cream. Whiz until smooth and creamy. Tip into a jug and store in the fridge for 24 hours.
2 When ready to cook, preheat the oven to 200°C, Gas 6. Grease six 10cm diameter Yorkshire pudding tins or round straight-sided tartlet tins with soft butter.
3 Halve the apricots and remove the stones. Cut each half in half, then divide among the prepared tins. Sift over some icing sugar. Pour in the batter, and bake for 12 minutes or until risen and lightly firm.
4 Cool for a few minutes in the tins, then unmould onto a wire tray using a small palette knife. Serve warm, dusted with a little more sifted icing sugar and scoops of icecream or spoonfuls of crème fraîche.

White chocolate and lemon mousse

Yellow and white are the colours I associate most with spring – like scented jaunty jonquils and comely white tulips. The rich puddings of winter make way for lighter textures and tastes. Instead of delicious dark chocolate mousses, I opt for a creamy white chocolate mixture tingling with zesty lemon. To continue the lemon theme, I suggest serving this with confit lemon slices. The mousse can be served scooped into quenelles with dessertspoons, or set in pretty ramekins or elegant wine glasses. I leave the size of portion to you – it's often nicer to serve small portions of a mousse after a good dinner. Less is more enjoyable, I always say. Note that this contains lightly cooked eggs. SERVES **4–6**

225g white chocolate, broken in pieces
3 large egg yolks
50g icing sugar
grated zest of 1 lemon
500ml double cream
Confit of Orange and Lemon (page 215, but made using
   all lemon slices instead of orange and lemon)

1 Melt the chocolate in a heatproof bowl set over a pan of barely simmering water. (We cover the bowl with cling film, but you may prefer to put a plate on top.) Alternatively, you can melt the chocolate in the microwave, on a low heat. Take care when melting though, as white chocolate can 'seize' more quickly than dark because of its lack of cocoa solids. When melted, stir and cool.
2 Whisk the egg yolks and sugar in another heatproof bowl set over the same saucepan of simmering water. You will need to make a firm sabayon foam, so an electric mixer will be a good bet. The mixture is ready when you can swirl a foam trail that holds its shape on the surface. Remove from the pan of water and cool for 10 minutes, whisking once or twice.
3 Carefully fold the melted chocolate and lemon zest into the sabayon. Cool and then lightly chill, but make sure it doesn't set. It must still be quite soft when you add the cream.
4 Whip the cream until it holds soft peaks, then fold into the chocolate mixture, one third at a time, using a palette knife. If serving in small dishes or glasses, divide the mousse among them. Chill until firm.
5 If serving as quenelles on dessert plates, place small spoonfuls of confit alongside. For ramekins or glasses, simply top each with a little confit.

Fresh apple parfait

This recipe is made in three stages – a creamy custard base, a meringue and an apple cream – which are combined and then frozen. It is an ideal dinner party dessert. Be sure to use a good-quality apple juice – those made by country firms such as James White from Suffolk have a wonderful flavour. Or, if you have an electric juicer, you can crush your own juice using full-flavoured Granny Smith or Cox's apples. Liquid glucose, which helps to stabilise the mixture, can be bought from chemists. Note that this contains lightly cooked egg yolks and raw egg whites. SERVES **8**

1 litre unsweetened apple juice
4 free-range egg yolks
225g caster sugar
3 tablespoons liquid glucose
3 egg whites
300ml double cream

1 Boil the apple juice until reduced to 300ml. Remove from the heat, cool and chill.
2 Heat a medium saucepan of water to boiling. Beat the egg yolks in a heatproof bowl that will fit over the saucepan. In another pan, heat 150g of the sugar, the liquid glucose and 4 tablespoons water until on the point of boiling. Pour this gradually onto the yolks, whisking with a balloon whisk.
3 Set the bowl over the boiling water and turn the heat to medium. Cook, stirring frequently, until thickened. Remove and cool.
4 Whisk the egg whites until softly stiff, then gradually whisk in the remaining caster sugar until you have a firm and glossy meringue.
5 Whip the cream to firm, soft peaks, then whisk in the reduced apple juice.
6 Combine all three parts, folding together with a large metal spoon. Scoop into a long terrine of at least 1kg capacity, then freeze until solid.
7 To serve, thaw for 10 minutes, then cut into slices.

Note: A fresh green *jus* of Granny Smith apples would be a delicate accompaniment. Core 2 apples, then whiz in a food processor with a squeeze of lemon juice. Strain, and trickle round each slice of parfait.

Rhubarb cheesecake with rhubarb compote

At the beginning of spring, you can buy long, slender stems of tender rhubarb in a day-glo pink colour. It needs little preparation except chopping into short lengths. Here it is pan-roasted and left to cool to a butterscotch-flavoured compote. This is spooned on top of a light cheesecake mousse set on a crisp base of crushed biscuits – one of my favourites, Hob Nobs! In the restaurant, we set this as baby cheesecakes in special deep moulds, lining the sides with thin bâtons of peeled rhubarb first blanched in hot stock syrup. The cheesecake here is a simpler version, but just as delicious. SERVES **6**

200ml double cream, lightly whipped
250g pack Hob Nobs (or digestive biscuits)
75g unsalted butter
2 teaspoons clear honey
100g cream cheese
100g crème fraîche
3–4 tablespoons caster sugar
grated zest of 1 lime
2 teaspoons lime juice

Compote
400g young pink rhubarb
50g unsalted butter
100g caster sugar
1 vanilla pod, slit open down the centre
sprigs fresh mint, to decorate (optional)

1 First, make the compote. Wash the rhubarb, pat dry and trim off the base of the stalks. Chop the rest into 4cm lengths.

2 Heat the butter in a non-stick frying pan and, when hot, quickly toss in the rhubarb pieces. Stir in the sugar and cook for about 5 minutes over a gentle heat until the rhubarb feels tender when pierced, but still keeps a good shape.

3 Meanwhile, scrape the seeds from the slit vanilla pod and mix with the double cream for the cheesecake. Set aside. Add the pod 'shell' to the rhubarb compote, then leave it to cool and take on a vanilla flavour. Chill.

4 Crush the biscuits to fine crumbs in a food processor. Or place in a thick plastic food bag, twist the top to seal and gently bash with a rolling pin to crumbs. Don't wallop it too hard or the bag might burst.

5 Melt the butter with the honey in a saucepan, tip in the crumbs and stir well until evenly mixed. Shake the mixture into a 21–23cm springform cake tin. Bat down the crumbs to compress, using the back of a spoon, and press well up the sides. Chill until firm.

6 Whiz the cream cheese, crème fraîche and sugar with the lime zest and juice in a food processor until creamy. Scoop out into a mixing bowl. Whip the vanilla-flavoured cream until softly stiff – that is, the cream forms soft peaks. Take care not to over-whip. Fold the cream into the cheese mixture and spoon into the prepared biscuit base. Chill to firm.

7 Spoon the compote over the cheesecake just as you are about to serve, removing the vanilla pod beforehand. Alternatively, you can put a spoonful of compote on each plate next to a slice of cheesecake and decorate with mint sprigs.

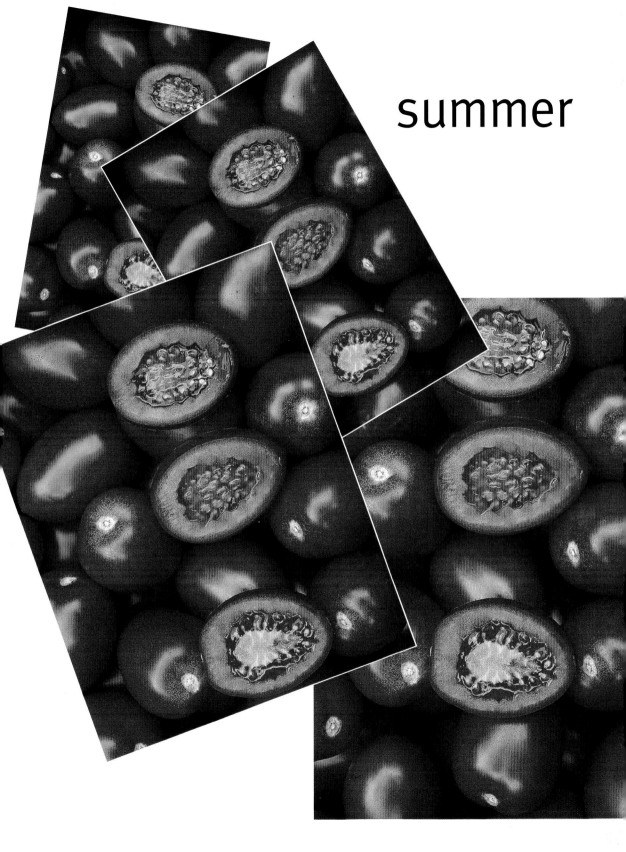

summer

For me, summer begins mid-May. In fact, by the third week of May I'm well into the swing, because we are sited next to the Chelsea Flower Show and that, as every devotee of the social scene will tell you, is very definitely the start of the summer season. Lunch during Chelsea week is unbelievably manic, but we are graced with some very elegant guests – and lovely hats!

Let's start with **tomatoes**, which are full of tremendous flavour from all the early summer heat. We use mainly plum tomatoes (the best come from Italy) and home-grown cherry tomatoes on the vine. We like to stuff plum tomatoes with finely chopped ratatouille to serve alongside grilled fish such as red mullet or pan-fried cannons of baby lamb. As a young commis in Paris, I remember being gobsmacked by one of Guy Savoy's starters – plum tomato halves filled with shredded braised oxtail and then gratinéed. It was perfection, the sharp, fruity tomato cutting the richness of the oxtail.

Cherry tomatoes have made a great difference to our cooking. Not only do they have an excellent flavour, but also the wonderful red of their skins means we seldom have to add any tomato purée to a stock or stew to pump up the colour.

Cherry tomatoes make great soups, delicious with thin floats of mozzarella *di bufala*, as well as a punchy gazpacho sauce and a tomato vinaigrette.

For a clever garnish, you might want to try making tomato *tuiles* or 'crisps'. It's really easy, but you do need to use an oven that has a very low setting – almost a plate-warming temperature. Failing that, you can prop open the oven door with a wooden spoon. All you do is thinly slice very firm, bright red plum or beef tomatoes with a serrated knife, lay the slices on a silicone cooking liner on a baking tray, and sprinkle with sea salt and black pepper. Then simply dry out in the low oven for a good few hours until the tomatoes are firm and you can peel them off the liner. Timing depends on your oven. In ours, it takes 12–16 hours on a pilot light (few domestic ovens have such things now). The first time you make them, start them in the morning and check after 4 hours, then thereafter every hour or so. Once they are dry, lay them on a wire rack to cool and crisp further.

Around Chelsea time we start to get in supplies of my favourite summer food, the kidney-shaped **Jersey Royal new potatoes**. I could happily sit and eat a bowl of them on their own, as they have so much flavour. From a cook's point of view, you can really do a lot with them because of their waxy texture. They make a good pomme purée, using the larger sizes – bake them on a bed of rock salt (to maintain the waxiness), peel while still warm (wearing rubber gloves, which we affectionately call our 'Marigolds') and then put through a potato ricer. We also crush boiled Jerseys against the side of a pan and mix in olive oil, chopped olives and tomatoes, to make *pommes écrasées*.

And they are brilliant sautéed in olive oil or goose fat. The skins of Jersey Royals are so delicate that they only need to be lightly scrubbed if serving whole – plain boiled or warm in salads (for the simplest, just toss them whilst hot in some vinaigrette). A great potato salad is Jerseys mixed with a little home-made mayonnaise (thinned down slightly with cream or more vinaigrette) and chopped spring/salad onions and topped with chopped fresh parsley or chervil. Jersey Royals have such a short season – about six to eight weeks (they can't be grown anywhere else) – so we really make the most of them.

I don't know who first had the brilliant idea to try cooking with **courgette flowers**, but I am grateful for the source of inspiration. As an ingredient, they are truly versatile, with an enchanting fragile beauty. We are supplied flowers with tiny wee vegetables, the length of my little finger, still attached. I know you cannot buy them easily, but home gardeners will find them simple to grow, so courgette flowers need not be thought of as elitist. In France, speciality growers insert thin plastic cups into the emerging flowers so the petals grow into a cup shape. This makes the mature flower the perfect shape for stuffing.

I use courgette flowers in two ways, always with the baby vegetable still attached. For the first, the flowers are filled with a light *farci* or stuffing, such as a mousse, a finely diced ratatouille or even a spicy cous cous, and then steamed over an aromatic simmering stock. I serve them with a delicate *jus* of Jerusalem artichokes or light velouté sauce. My other favourite is to gently slit one side of the flower and open it up like a sheet of paper,

then dip it into the lightest *beignet* or fritter batter and deep-fry for a minute or two in hot olive oil, to serve tempura-style with a little freshly made chilli jam.

Another summer favourite is wild **girolle** mushrooms (aka chanterelles), which we get mostly from France, although increasingly (I'm thrilled to say) from Scotland. Their warm golden-yellow colour adds a touch of luxury to our dishes. We tend to use the smaller ones for garnishing and serving with dishes. The larger ones are sautéed and served with mussels in a cream sauce, or made into a girolles *duxelles* to stir into fish veloutés. Girolles do need to be prepared carefully – thoroughly rinsed to remove all grit, and then left to dry completely. When girolles are plentiful, my young commis are shown how to pickle them for the rest of the season (turn to page 213 for instructions).

After my time in Paris, I had a job cooking on a boat in the South of France, where I learnt about **black olives** firsthand. Whenever I could, I would make my way to the olive market in old Nice, to talk to the olive farmers, or should I say listen to them talking, because they were passionate about their fruits. In the restaurant we only use black olives from Nice. They are neat perfect fruits, and need very little added to them – no garlic, lemon or chilli. Finely chopped and mixed into a tapenade, we place them as quenelles on top of grilled salmon. We also sprinkle them on lamb niçoise or stir them into a fresh ratatouille. I find I can't stop myself from nibbling them on their own.

Another favourite from my time in the Mediterranean is fresh spriggy **thyme**, particularly lemon thyme. I use it in a variety of ways, all year round (there is no need to resort to using dried thyme because it is generally easy to get hold of). In summer, thyme has an especially good zing, and a host of savoury and sweet dishes benefit from its presence. We pick off the tips of the sprigs, which we call 'flowers', and sprinkle them over lamb whilst it is roasting, over plump scallops and over sautéed new potatoes. We almost always use thyme in marinades and tie it up in bouquets garnis. We use it in sweet crème brûlées and even infused in the custard base for icecream.

You can always tell when a food has become hip, because supermarkets start to sell their own versions. Some years ago it became fashionable to use edible flowers in salads, and for a time you could buy mixed salads with flowers. Fashions bloom and then fade, but we still enjoy using flowers in cooking, chiefly to infuse creamy mixtures such as custards or a rich chocolate ganache. The two flowers I enjoy using at the moment are jasmine and lavender. Both have light floral fragrances that add an inspired touch of mystery – even my regular diners can't guess the elegant flavour. We serve **jasmine** in a consommé, crystallise the dainty flowers for pastries, and use it to subtly enhance the flavours of a tea sorbet made with Earl Grey. While jasmine is used fresh, **lavender** flowers are best dried to concentrate the flavour and then rubbed to separate them from the stalks. We crush the flowers to mix (sparingly) into shortbreads or sprinkle them onto a rich bread dough before baking.

Two spices remind me of summer, even in the deepest winter – saffron and cinnamon. Both have a great depth of flavour and both need to be used sparingly, otherwise your dish will suffer from overkill. Less is definitely more with them. It's important to ensure that **saffron** is very dry so the strands can be crushed into a powder with just fingers. We sprinkle saffron on the skin of fish such as red mullet, just a pinch per fish, then leave to marinate for 5 minutes or so. This allows the saffron flavour to permeate the flesh, and the skin cooks to a deep golden-red. We also use saffron in mussel soup, with leeks, and to give an exotic flavour and rich colour to pasta dough (first make a concentrated essence by crushing strands into a little boiling water, then shake a few drops into the dough as you knead it smooth). Saffron is classic in risottos and pilaffs (again, just a pinch or two), but have you ever tried it in icecream? It's wonderful. Infuse strands in the cream and milk for the custard base before churning smooth.

You can make fantastic icecream with **cinnamon** too, and it is wonderful in syrups for fruits such as apples and pears. But to my mind, the fruit that is made to be flattered by cinnamon is the black fig, which comes to us from Egypt in the late summer. We also use cinnamon, along with Chinese five-spice, in rich red wine sauces to serve with full-flavoured or firm-textured fish like brill or turbot.

Although the French boast about the freshness of Brittany **lobsters**, in the top Paris restaurants where I worked, the lobsters actually came from Scotland. Today, I always try to use lobsters that have been trapped in the clear loch-fed waters of the west of Scotland. If they are scarce, we use Canadian lobsters. When preparing lobsters a good rule to follow is: the more it costs, the less you need to do to it. One of my first signature dishes was roasted lobster with vanilla, simple but superb. In summer we poach lobsters in a court bouillon, then serve them on a spicy guacamole, with a fine clear tomato consommé. Lobsters are naturally vicious creatures and attack each other, pulling off claws if they can. As we often chop the meat for ravioli fillings, I buy what the trade calls 'cripples', which are minus one claw, occasionally two. The tail meat is still succulent and tasty, although the clawless lobster is a sorry sight.

I have a confession to make: I judge the ability of any new commis chef who starts in my kitchen by the skill he or she displays in opening the wonderful scallops delivered to our kitchens each day. Such beautiful food is pricey, and we cannot afford to make mistakes. We take only hand-dived scallops from the west of Scotland. They are delivered so fresh, they pulsate as we open them. This is not an easy task, as the shells are clamped very tightly shut. I tell new recruits that the secret is to be very cunning. It's man against muscle. Stick the tip of the knife only into the hinge and sever the muscle that holds both shells together. Once this is done you can feel the scallop relax, and the two shells can be prised open. Then put the knife tip under the scallop and its frilly skirt in the rounded shell and gently ease it all away, including the coral. (We don't use the corals, except to sometimes dry them out in a low oven overnight, then grind to a fine powder, for flavouring risottos or using in sauces.)

Scallops come in various sizes. Ours generally weigh in at around 50g after cleaning, without the corals. Much bigger than this, they hold too much water and can be tough. The very freshest scallops are used raw, chopped into a *tartare*. My favourite way of cooking scallops is dusted with spices and sautéed, then tossed with baby new potatoes to make a warm salad.

The smaller queen scallops are ideal for risottos and mixed salads. They are a bit of a pain to open, but we find a butter knife helps with the shell and a teaspoon with detaching the scallop. Reared in warmer waters than 'king' scallops, the queens have a slightly sweeter flavour.

Fishing has been one of my great passions ever since I was a small boy, when my father would take my brother and me up to the Scottish lochs to fish. In early summer I itch to find time to catch wild salmon as they return to their spawning patches on the River Dee. After an incredible swim of thousands of miles, the flesh of these magnificent fish is muscular, full of flavour and a rich dark pink from their natural diet. Their tails and fins have an incredible span when compared to their less fortunate farmed kith and kin, and the heads taper to a pronounced hook nose, which they use to burrow under pebbles and rocks seeking food and shelter. Modern-day fishermen have the benefit of sophisticated underwater photo technology, which can chart the progress and size of the salmon as they swim home. And that is wonderful to watch.

Such perfect natural food needs very little embellishment from me – just neat trimming and simple grilling or pan-frying, 95 per cent of the time on the skin side, which should cook to an appetising crispness. Wild salmon and cod are the only fish I season a good 20 minutes ahead of time, to draw moisture from the skin and enhance the flavour just a tad. Sometimes, I score the skin and spike it with tips of thyme sprigs, then rub the skin with olive oil.

I have quite a fondness for good caviar (I'm sure that comes as no surprise). My favourite is known as 'golden caviar', from the albino Caraburun sturgeon. In the restaurant we use mainly Osietra, with its firm texture and nutty flavour, and Sevruga, which is ideal for sauces and garnishes. It takes several years for a sturgeon to reach the size when the eggs are ideal for caviar, which is one reason it is so expensive. It is not always easy to get good value for money when buying caviar, and, although sold packed in cans, the quality can vary enormously. The eggs can be bruised or oily or the flavour can taste flat. The best way of ensuring the best quality is to buy from a good supplier. My favourite brand is Imperial Caviar UK, which is run by an Iranian friend, Ramin Rohgar. Much has been written about the poor quality control of certain caviar suppliers and the problems of overfishing (once caught, the fish cannot be returned to the sea to continue growing). The Iranians have the better quality controls because their political system is more stable. Also, the sturgeons in the south of the Caspian Sea are larger and not subject to overfishing. Caviar features on our menus with poached lobster and folded into crème fraîche as a garnish. We also fold it into scrambled eggs and fish veloutés and mix it with sea urchin butter. But, so it is said, the best way of eating caviar is from a mother-of-pearl shell with a fine mother-of-pearl spoon.

Even in summer, many of our clients enjoy a nice piece of steak, often with a

light sauce such as creamed parsley purée and sautéed summer girolles. A favourite cut of mine is **ribeye of beef**. Popular for years in Scotland, it is now appearing on menus 'down south'. It is just as good as fillet for tenderness with, I think, more flavour. It takes just minutes to cook on or off the bone (on the bone it is the classic T-bone steak). We buy ribeye in a large piece, wrap it tightly in cling film and refrigerate for a good 24 hours to 'set' the shape, before cutting it into even-size steaks.

Summer isn't summer without **peaches**. My favourite ones are the white-flesh varieties from Italy, which reach our suppliers from May onwards. Later on, firm and juicy yellow peaches appear. While there is little to beat a perfect fresh peach served simply sliced, peaches are a very versatile ingredient and we capitalise on this in our kitchen, for both sweet and savoury dishes. At the height of gluts, we make Kilner jars of peach chutney (see the recipe on page 213) to serve as a relish with fresh foie gras, pâté and butter-roasted chicken, and with cheese and walnut bread. Pan-fried peaches glazed with sugar and vinegar are memorable with duck, goose or lamb.

One of my favourite ways of serving peaches is to marry the sweet succulent flesh with aromatic thyme, a herb that seems to cut the richness of the peach flavour and heighten the fruitiness. It's a combination that works well for peaches simply poached in a thyme-flavoured sugar syrup and for peaches served with a home-made thyme icecream.

We also make light, crisp peach *tuiles*, by slicing just ripe and firm fruit wafer-thin, brushing with stock syrup and oven-drying for a few hours. To get the roof-tile shape, we press the dried slices over a rolling pin and leave them to crisp. Peach *tuiles* are a very pretty garnish for creamy puddings.

In mid- to late summer our supplies of **figs** come in from Italy. These beautiful plump, dark-skinned fruits with a downy surface and pert little hooked tips have quite a short season, so we use them every way we can. You have to judge the ripeness fairly exactly. If underripe, they leak a white milkiness; if too ripe, they become squashy. I love to roast them whole with a balsamic-flavoured caramel or simply with sugar, butter and cinnamon. They can be simmered into a chunky chutney, delicious with foie gras. We also slice firm fruits wafer-thin and dry them as *tuiles*. One of my creations is fig *carpaccio*, which is embarrassingly simple to make. Take firm fruit and peel thinly, removing the tips, then cut in half and scoop out the seeds. Lay the halves between large sheets of cling film and bat with a rolling pin until very thin. Don't whack too hard, just enough to flatten thinly and evenly. Then freeze and keep like this until ready to serve. Remove from the freezer, peel off the cling film and place directly on a large flat dinner plate. Top with a coarse pâté, like the Mosaic of Autumn Game on page 130, or some heavenly slices of pan-fried foie gras. What more can I say?

In the early days of the Aubergine restaurant, we were very daring and gave our guests ripe fresh **cherries** nestled in bowls of crushed ice instead of petits fours. The idea went down a storm, as the juicy fruitiness cleared satiated palates perfectly. At the height of summer, we get luscious dark red cherries from Spain, and I really enjoy working my way through a pile of them. At other times of the year, growers in Italy, America, Chile and South Africa fly us in beautifully sweet fruits. Cherries are good in both sweet and savoury dishes. They make a classic partnership with duck breasts, and I like them with caramel and balsamic sauce. You can use them in a dessert soup too, as well as for fresh cherry icecream (stone and crush about 300g cherries, then blend with a rich crème anglaise and churn in an icecream machine). Great with almondy biscuits.

I know **chocolate** is not a seasonal food, but I associate it with summer because I like to combine it with the heady fragrance of lavender flowers. I was introduced to the idea of combining chocolate and lavender by a talented French chocolatier whom I met whilst cooking as a guest chef at the Singapore Raffles. Such a 'marriage' of flavours isn't really surprising, of course – from the early days of chocolate-making in Europe, cooks have enhanced chocolate with flowery flavours. Examples are rose, as found in chocolate-coated Turkish delight bars, and violet, geranium and other flower creams in chocolate boxes. Dark, milk and white chocolate all benefit from the lavender connection. With white chocolate, we like to melt the chocolate slowly, even overnight, over a warm hot cupboard, with a healthy-sized sprig or two of lavender flowerheads to give their perfume. The next day the lavender is strained or spooned out, leaving its flowery fragrance in the chocolate.

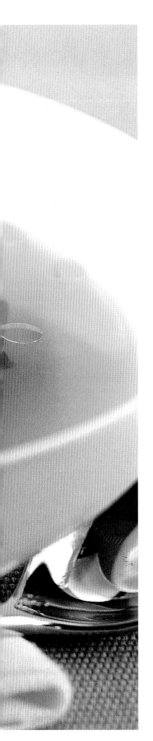

Light tomato broth with a paysanne of vegetables

This is a version of a tomato consommé we serve in the restaurant with baby lobster tails. As a chilled summer soup it is unsurpassed. I guarantee you will not taste such a full, fresh tomato flavour anywhere, yet it looks as clear and bright as a glass of sparkling wine. The dainty floating garnish flaunts the choicest summer vegetables. **SERVES 4 AS A STARTER**

2 large shallots, chopped

4 tablespoons olive oil, plus extra for serving

1kg ripe plum tomatoes, roughly chopped

2 cloves garlic, sliced

1 teaspoon fine sea salt

1 teaspoon sugar

1 teaspoon each chopped fresh basil,
   chervil and tarragon

4 free-range egg whites

¼ teaspoon each white peppercorns
   and black peppercorns

50g mangetouts, trimmed

50g fine green beans, topped and tailed

about 20 asparagus tips

1 Sweat the shallots in 3 tablespoons of the oil for 3 minutes until softened, then stir in three-quarters of the chopped tomatoes, the garlic, sea salt, sugar and the herbs. Cook over a medium heat for about 10 minutes, stirring occasionally, until a little pulpy.

2 Pour in 1 litre water and bring to the boil. Simmer for about 20 minutes, skimming the surface of any froth with a large spoon.

3 Line a colander with a large wet piece of muslin or thin clean tea towel and set over a basin. Pour the tomato liquid through the colander, pressing down on the debris with the back of a ladle. Chill the liquid by standing the basin in a bowl of iced water.

4 Whiz the remaining chopped tomatoes with the egg whites and peppercorns in a food processor. Tip into a large saucepan and add the strained tomato liquid.

5 Bring the contents of the pan slowly to the boil and simmer for 20 minutes. You should notice the liquid becoming crystal clear as it bubbles.

6 Rinse out the muslin or tea towel and place back in the colander set over a bowl. Slowly pour the liquid into the lined colander – it should run through beautifully clear. If it does not, slowly pour it back through the colander set over another bowl. Chill until ready to serve.

7 To make the garnish, cut the mangetouts in diamonds. Heat the remaining tablespoon of oil in a small frying pan and gently fry the mangetouts, beans and asparagus tips for about 3 minutes until just wilted. Drain on kitchen paper towel.

8 Scatter the mangetouts, beans and asparagus into four large soup bowls. Pour over the clear broth. If you like, you can drizzle over some extra virgin olive oil, then serve straightaway.

Pepper and tomato soup with crab cocktail

A soup does not have to be brimming with liquid and a miscellany of floating diced solids. Sometimes I like to create a centrepiece of a mixture like this seafood cocktail and surround it with a light, flavoursome broth. Choose ripe, plum tomatoes for this recipe. If you wish to give the pepper more kick, grill or roast it first. Fresh crab is best, as it is less watery than frozen and has a sweeter flavour than canned. In the colder winter months you could use lobster meat instead of crab. SERVES 4 AS A STARTER

3 tablespoons olive oil, plus
   extra for drizzling
2 large red peppers, about 500g
   total weight, chopped
6 large, ripe plum tomatoes, about 500g
   total weight, chopped
4 shallots, chopped
about 12 leaves fresh basil
1 sprig fresh thyme
1 small bay leaf
800ml tomato juice
100ml double cream
250g fresh white crab meat

1 Granny Smith apple, peeled,
   cored and finely diced
1 baby Cos or romaine lettuce,
   finely shredded
1 ripe avocado
sea salt and freshly ground black pepper

Sauce
4–6 tablespoons Mayonnaise (page 213)
1 tablespoon tomato purée
a few drops of hot pepper sauce
juice of 1 lime

1 Heat the oil in a large saucepan, then add the peppers, tomatoes, shallots and herbs. Sauté gently for about 5 minutes, then stir, cover and leave to cook gently for 10 minutes.
2 Uncover, and remove the thyme and bay leaf. Stir in the tomato juice and cream, season well and allow to cool. Whiz in a food processor or blender until smooth and creamy, scraping down the sides once or twice. Rub through a sieve into a bowl, using the back of a ladle. Chill the soup for a good 2 hours.
3 Meanwhile, check the crab with a fork for any flecks of shell and cartilage, which can be so irritating to bite on in the middle of a dream dish. Put in a bowl with the apple and lettuce.
4 For the sauce, beat the mayonnaise with the tomato purée, pepper sauce, half the lime juice and some seasoning. Mix just enough into the crab to make a nice firm but moist mixture.
5 Crush the avocado with a fork. Add the remaining lime juice and some seasoning.
6 Check the soup for seasoning. (Chilled foods need more seasoning than hot ones.)
7 Set a plain scone cutter, about 5cm in diameter, in the middle of a wide soup bowl. Spoon a quarter of the avocado into the base of the cutter, then add a quarter of the crab mix over that. (See photographs of this technique on page 221.) Finally, nappé the top of the crab with a little of the remaining cocktail sauce, and carefully lift off the cutter. Repeat with three other bowls.
8 Pour the soup around each crab cocktail, add a drizzle of oil if you like, and serve immediately.

Aubergine and pepper soup with sautéed cherry tomatoes

This chilled summer soup uses twice-roasted aubergines and peppers. It is an unusual recipe that bursts with Mediterranean flavour. Small servings could be given as a starter, or larger ones for a light main meal with warm French bread or ciabatta. **Serves 6 as a starter or 4 as a light main dish**

4 medium aubergines

leaves from 1 sprig fresh rosemary

1 tablespoon chopped garlic,
   preferably new season's

olive oil, for frying

2 large red peppers

2 large yellow peppers

1 shallot, chopped

2 sprigs fresh basil

1 tablespoon coarsegrain mustard

300ml Vegetable Nage (page 212)
   or Light Chicken Stock (page 212)

about 250ml tomato juice (optional)

about 200g cherry tomatoes on the vine

sea salt and freshly ground black pepper

1 Preheat the oven to 190°C, Gas 5. Peel the skin from the aubergines in long strips using a swivel vegetable peeler, taking about 5mm of flesh still attached to the skin. Cut the skin into thin strips and then into small dice. Set aside.

2 Wrap the peeled aubergines in foil with the rosemary leaves and garlic. Roast for about 45 minutes or until the flesh has completely broken down and softened. Save the cooking juices.

3 Heat about 2 tablespoons of olive oil in a large frying pan and, when hot, cook the soft aubergine flesh over a high heat to give it a slightly scorched flavour. Mix in the saved roasting juices and season. Remove from the pan and set aside to cool.

4 Stand the peppers upright on a board and cut the flesh from the central seed core and stalk. (This is a good tip – it stops the seeds flying everywhere.) Chop the pepper flesh.

5 Add another tablespoon or two of oil to the frying pan and, when hot, sauté the shallot until lightly coloured. Mix in the peppers and continue frying over a high heat for about 5 minutes. Mix in the basil and mustard, then the vegetable nage or stock. Bring to the boil and season, then simmer for 12–15 minutes. Remove from the heat and cool.

6 Discard the basil, then pour the pepper mixture into a food processor or blender. Add the aubergine and whiz until smooth and creamy. The soup will be quite thick. If you want it thinner, then gradually mix in tomato juice. Chill until ready to serve.

7 To prepare the garnish, heat a little oil in the frying pan and fry the reserved chopped aubergine skin until light and crisp. Take care not to overbrown. Drain on kitchen paper towel.

8 Add a tad more oil to the pan and heat it. Pull the tomatoes from the stalks and fry them, just to flavour the skin. They will go a bit squashy, which is fine. Drain on kitchen paper towel.

9 Check the seasoning of the soup – it should be quite pungent and full flavoured – then pour into four to six chilled bowls. Divide the sautéed cherry tomatoes among the bowls and scatter over the crispy aubergine flakes.

Chilled cucumber soup with ribbons of smoked wild salmon

Little demi-tasse cups of a light cucumber soup are frequently served in the restaurant as an amuse-gueule – *an appetite-teaser. The secret to the depth of flavour lies in the marinating and the use of my light fragrant vegetable nage. Don't serve too much – keep the delicacy intact. Some fine slices of smoked wild salmon (as made by the established East London firm, Forman's) contrast prettily with the pastel green soup.* **SERVES 4–6 AS A STARTER**

2 large cucumbers, washed and dried
2 tablespoons creamed horseradish
500ml Vegetable Nage (page 212)
a small fistful of fresh mint stalks
200ml double cream
about 100g smoked wild salmon
sea salt and freshly ground black pepper

1 Cut off the ends of the cucumbers. Thinly slice them, complete with skin (which gives the soup its glorious colour). This can be done on a mandolin or using a slicer attachment on a food processor. Place in a large bowl.
2 Stir in the horseradish and vegetable nage with a little seasoning. Twist the mint stalks to release the flavour, then mix these in too. Cover and chill for 2 hours or so.
3 Remove the mint stalks, then whiz everything to a smooth purée in a food processor or blender. Pass the liquid through a fine sieve into a bowl, rubbing the pulp through with the back of a ladle. The soup should be quite thick. Whisk in the cream and check the seasoning – chilled soups should be well flavoured or they will disappoint.
4 Slice the salmon into thin strips and place in the centre of four to six soup bowls, depending on whether you want to serve a lot of soup or a daintier portion. Pour the chilled soup around and serve immediately.

Note: Instead of smoked salmon, you could try a little shredded smoked eel.

Sweetcorn and spring onion risotto

The Italians serve risotto as a starter, whilst the French often use it as an accompaniment to a main course. I find it really versatile, as it can also make a light main dish. The basic recipe is always the same – it's the flavour variations that give character. This is a light and refreshing dish using the first of the summer sweetcorn. Always buy sweetcorn cobs still dressed in their green husks – those sold wrapped in plastic, which you find in many supermarkets, will have lost their 'just picked' fresh juiciness. Instead of enriching the tender rice grains with mascarpone, I stir in a purée of creamed sweetcorn. SERVES 4 AS A STARTER OR 2 AS A MAIN DISH

500–600ml Vegetable Nage (page 212)
  or Light Chicken Stock (page 212)
1 large sweetcorn cob, still in its husk
1 shallot, finely chopped
3 tablespoons olive oil
200g risotto rice (Carnaroli, Arborio or Vialone Nano)
about 4 tablespoons dry white wine
2 spring onions, cut in thin rounds
200g can creamed sweetcorn
3 tablespoons freshly grated Parmesan cheese
a good knob of unsalted butter
sea salt and freshly ground black pepper

1 Put the nage or stock into a pan and heat to a gentle simmer.
2 Pull the green husks and the silky yellow threads from the corn cob. Stand the cob upright, tapered end down. Using a sharp heavy-bladed cook's knife, cut straight down the cob, releasing the small square kernels (see photograph of this technique on page 218). Discard the central core, and scoop the kernels into a bowl. (They might have popped out all over the worktop.)
3 In a large saucepan, gently sauté the shallot in 2 tablespoons of the oil for about 5 minutes until softened but not coloured. Stir in the remaining tablespoon of oil and the sweetcorn kernels. Cook for a minute or so, then add the rice and cook for a minute, stirring.
4 Pour in the wine and cook until it has reduced away, then ladle in a quarter of the nage or stock. Bring to the boil, stirring, then turn down to a medium heat and continue bubbling gently until the liquid has been absorbed. Spoon in another ladleful of nage or stock and repeat the process, still stirring. Continue adding liquid in ladlefuls, waiting for each batch to be absorbed and stirring often, until the rice is plump and just tender but not soft. This should take about 15 minutes. (You may not need all the nage or stock.)
5 Stir in the spring onions and cook for a minute or two to heat. Then gradually stir in the creamed corn, half the Parmesan and the butter. When hot, season well and serve immediately in shallow bowls, topped with more Parmesan.

A special salade niçoise

Fresh tuna is a must for this ultimate summer salad. I suggest you look for line-caught blue fin tuna, although yellow fin makes fine eating too. Ask for a loin cut, and avoid any fish with bruised flesh or blood lines. The recipe is quite straightforward, but I like to add a touch of luxury and use little quail's eggs instead of the usual quartered hen's ones. SERVES 4 AS A STARTER OR LIGHT DISH

12 quail's eggs

3 tablespoons white wine vinegar

100g thin French beans, topped
   and tailed, then halved if liked

150g baby new potatoes

100ml Classic Vinaigrette (page 213)
   mixed with 3 tablespoons double cream

4 firm plum tomatoes, skinned

50g salted anchovies (the ones sold loose)

50g fresh black olives

200g mixed baby salad leaves
   (such as the tips of frisée or oak leaf
   lettuce, wild rocket, baby Cos)

4 tuna loin steaks, about 100g each

1–2 tablespoons olive oil

1 tablespoon basalmic vinegar

sea salt and freshly ground black pepper

1 There are lots of stages for this recipe, so get everything prepared first. The cooked quail's eggs will be easier to peel if first soaked in cold water to cover, mixed with the 3 tablespoons vinegar, for 20 minutes. This breaks down the tough albumen in the shells. Then drain and cook for 2 minutes in boiling water. Drain and plunge into a bowl of cold water to cool for 10 minutes. Peel and leave whole.

2 Blanch the green beans in boiling water for 2 minutes, drain and refresh in ice-cold water. Drain again.

3 Cook the baby new potatoes for 12 minutes until just tender. Drain and toss in 2 tablespoons of the cream dressing. Leave to cool.

4 Quarter each tomato lengthways and scoop out the seeds. Leave them as petal shapes or slice in half again.

5 Rinse the anchovies in tepid water, then cut into a rough dice. Stone and slice the olives.

6 Pick over the salad leaves. Mix with the green beans and toss with the remaining dressing. Divide the leaves and beans among four large shallow bowls or dinner plates. Scatter over the anchovies, tomatoes and olives. Arrange the potatoes and eggs around the leaves.

7 Now cook the tuna steaks. Heat a large, heavy non-stick frying pan until you can feel a good heat rising. Add a little oil, then lay in the tuna steaks. Cook for 1–2 minutes on each side until they feel lightly springy when pressed. The tuna should still be pink in the centre. If you like yours more cooked, then allow longer, but don't cook too well done or the flesh will be dry and chewy. Deglaze with the basalmic vinegar. Season and lift out of the pan.

8 Cut each steak in half and lay on top of the waiting salads. Serve straightaway.

Scottish lobster with mango and spinach salad

This dish is a real treat for the eye – simply stunning colours of pink, gold and deep green.
I would advise that for the best flavour you cook your own lobsters (put them in the freezer first
to make them sleepy). Another useful hint is that it is easier to shell them whilst they are still
warm. **SERVES 4 AS A STARTER OR LIGHT DISH**

Court Bouillon (page 212)
4 small live lobsters, about 700g each
2 just ripe mangoes
3 tablespoons Classic Vinaigrette (page 213)
150g baby spinach leaves
sea salt and freshly ground black pepper

1 Bring the court bouillon to a gentle boil, then drop in the lobsters. Poach them gently for
5–6 minutes. Remove the pan from the heat and allow the lobsters to cool a little in the bouillon.
2 When the lobsters are cool enough for you to handle (wear rubber gloves), remove them and
take the meat from the shells. Use strong kitchen scissors or poultry shears to cut through the
body shell, and take out the meat in one piece. Check the third disc along for the dirt sac and
pull this out. Extract the meat from the claws and knuckles by cracking the shells with the back
of the knife. Chop the claw and knuckle meat. Pop all the shelled meat back into the bouillon
and leave to cool down and absorb more flavour. When cold, remove and drain.
3 Peel the mangoes, cut the flesh off the central stone and chop into small dice. Toss with
half the vinaigrette.
4 Toss the spinach leaves in the remaining vinaigrette and season well. Arrange the spinach
in the centre of four plates (we arrange ours in a petal pattern).
5 Scatter over the dressed mango. Put the lobster knuckle and claw meat in the centre.
Slice the lobster tail meat into medallions and arrange on top of the mango. Serve it as is.

Salad of queen scallops, baby calamari and confit new potatoes

Dainty, pretty and in a class of its own, this is an elegant starter for a special summer dinner. You need the very small baby calamari, sold ready cleaned with the tentacles pushed inside the bodies. The small queen scallops, which look quite enchanting in their little shells, are becoming more available in quality fishmongers. They are sometimes sold in nets, although some shops sell them ready shelled. If so, check they are not frozen, or the flesh will taste watery. For the potatoes, use little Jersey Royals, in their brief season, or try baby Ratte or Anya varieties. Incidentally, you can now buy goose fat in cans. Even my local supermarket sells it.

SERVES 4 AS A STARTER

200g baby new potatoes
  (the smaller the better)
100g goose fat
200ml tepid milk
120g plain flour
1 teaspoon easy-blend dried yeast
4 baby calamari, about 75g each
about 32–40 queen scallops,
  removed from their shells

a few good pinches of mild curry powder
some light olive oil, for frying
4–6 tablespoons Classic Vinaigrette (page 213)
  mixed with 2 teaspoons chopped fresh tarragon
about 300g mixed salad leaves (varieties with
  soft leaves such as mâche or oak leaf)
sea salt and freshly ground black pepper

1 First, confit the potatoes, which has to be done on a very low heat. You may find a metal heat diffuser useful. Put the potatoes and goose fat into a small saucepan – the potatoes should be covered in the fat. Cook on the lowest heat setting for 20–25 minutes until just tender. The fat may bubble occasionally, but don't let it get any hotter. The potatoes should cook, not fry. Drain on kitchen paper towel and cool. Save the fat.

2 Whiz the milk, flour, yeast and a good pinch of salt to a thick batter in a food processor or blender. Tip into a shallow bowl and set aside in the fridge for 1 hour.

3 Check the calamari are clean inside, then pat dry.

4 Season the scallops with a little salt, pepper and curry powder to coat. Heat 1 tablespoon of oil in a frying pan and, when hot, add the scallops and quickly toss for less than a minute. Remove and drain, then toss in half the vinaigrette. Set aside.

5 Halve the new potatoes. Heat a tablespoon of the saved goose fat in a frying pan. When hot, quickly brown the potatoes until crispy, then drain and season. Keep warm.

6 Pick over the salad leaves, season and toss with the remaining vinaigrette. Mound in the centre of four large plates.

7 Heat about 1cm of oil in a frying pan. Remove the batter from the fridge and dip in the calamari bodies and tentacles, coating evenly. Lay them in the hot oil and cook for a couple of minutes on each side until crispy and golden. Do not overcook. Drain and season.

8 Spoon the scallops on top of the salad and sit the calamari on top of that. Arrange the potatoes around the salad and serve.

Tartare of scallops and golden caviar with tomato jus

Because our scallops are so fresh, they are perfect for delicate and creamy tartares, which are simple and pure in flavour. However, when gently blended with a spoonful of the rare Imperial caviar they become exquisite. Imperial caviar (aka Golden Osietra), the roe of the albino Caraburun sturgeon, is a brilliant gold colour with a mild, almost nutty flavour. My occasional supply comes from Imperial Caviar UK, run by a great friend, Ramin Rohgar. You buy it in 50g cans. Use half in the tartare and the rest delicately balanced on top as a glistening garnish. The jus *served around the tartare is made from the extract of fresh tomatoes left to drip overnight – suprisingly it is clear and gives no indication of the food origin until you sip it. Quite, quite clever, I think.* **SERVES 4 AS A STARTER**

400g ripe plum tomatoes
2 large leaves fresh basil
8 very fresh, large king scallops,
   removed from their shells, without corals
1 tablespoon crème fraîche
1 tablespoon mascarpone
1 teaspoon chopped fresh chervil
1 teaspoon chopped fresh chives
juice of ¹/₂ lime (approximately)
50g Imperial caviar
sea salt

1 First, make the tomato *jus*. Chop the tomatoes roughly, then whiz in a food processor with the basil and a little salt for just a few seconds to a chunky purée. Tip into a clean jelly bag that is held suspended above a bowl. Allow the juice to drip through overnight. The liquid will run clear.
2 Now, if you wish, you could boil the juice down to reduce it by half and concentrate the flavour, but then it won't taste as fresh. Chill the *jus*.
3 For the tartare, chop the scallops very, very finely by hand, then mix with the crème fraîche, mascarpone, herbs and salt. Drop by drop, add lime juice, tasting as you go, until you feel it's sufficient. Gently fold in half the caviar.
4 Place a 4–5cm plain cutter in the middle of a small shallow bowl. Spoon in a quarter of the tartare and level the top lightly. Lift off the cutter, and repeat with three other bowls.
5 Spoon the remaining caviar on top of each tartare as a garnish. Serve lightly chilled, with the tomato *jus* in a separate little jug to drizzle around the mounds.

Summery quails in a tomato tarragon dressing

Quails look so inviting with their small plump breasts. Many people find them fiddly to eat, so we remove the breasts after roasting and cool them in a light tomato dressing. They are served on a warm salad of celery and summer girolles. A terrific starter. **SERVES 4 AS A STARTER**

4 fresh quails

6 tablespoons olive oil

½ small tomato, seeded
   and very finely chopped

½ shallot, very finely chopped

½ teaspoon tomato ketchup

½ teaspoon coarsegrain mustard

½ teaspoon fresh lemon juice

1 teaspoon chopped fresh tarragon

4 small sticks celery, cut into small lengths

100ml Chicken Stock (page 212)
   or Vegetable Nage (page 212)

70g fresh girolles, ends trimmed,
   then halved if large

a few celery leaves, to garnish
   (can be deep-fried, if liked)

sea salt and freshly ground black pepper

1 Preheat the oven to 190°C, Gas 5. Brush the quails lightly with a little of the oil, season and roast for 12 minutes.

2 Meanwhile, make a dressing by mixing together the finely chopped tomato, shallot, ketchup, mustard, lemon juice, tarragon and 3 tablespoons of the oil. Season well.

3 Remove the quails from the oven and allow to stand for 10 minutes. Using a sharp boning knife, remove the lightly cooked breasts, keeping them whole. (Use the carcasses in a stock.) Mix the breasts into the tomato dressing and set aside to cool.

4 Heat 1 tablespoon of the remaining oil in a small frying pan and sauté the celery until golden brown. Pour in the stock or nage, season nicely and cover the celery with a butter paper. Simmer for about 10 minutes until softened and the liquid has evaporated away.

5 Meanwhile, sauté the girolles in the last of the oil for about 5 minutes, stirring once or twice, then season.

6 To serve, place the celery in the centre of four dinner plates. Spoon the girolles on top. Arrange the quail breasts on top of that and trickle around any leftover dressing. Garnish with celery leaves.

Linguine in lobster and girolle sauce

This is something of a classic dish (with sauce américaine), and you will need time and patience to make it. But it is certainly worth it. It is best to buy live lobster for this dish, as you need to sauté the shells to give a good colour to the sauce. Buy the linguine fresh if you can, from a good Italian store. **SERVES 4 AS A STARTER**

2 live lobsters, about 700g each
a little olive oil, for frying
1 small carrot, finely diced
1 small leek, finely diced
1 small onion, finely chopped
1 small stick celery, finely diced
2 tablespoons Pernod
100ml dry white wine
1 medium tomato, chopped
2 teaspoons tomato purée

500ml Fish Stock (page 212)
  or Light Chicken Stock (page 212)
250ml double cream
2 large leaves fresh basil
120g fresh girolles, ends trimmed
25g butter
leaves from a small bunch of fresh
  flat-leaf parsley, chopped
300g fresh linguine
sea salt and freshly ground black pepper

1 First, prepare the lobsters. Freeze them for 30 minutes so they become sleepy. Bring a large pan of water to the boil and drop in the lobsters. Leave for a minute, then remove from the water and cool until you can handle them. Pull off the head and claws. Extract the meat from the body shell using sharp scissors or poultry shears to cut through. The meat will still be raw, but sufficiently loosened for you to pull it out. Extract the meat from the claws. Set the meat aside.

2 Smash the lobster shells a bit so they will fit into a large pan. Heat 2–3 tablespoons of oil in the pan and sauté the shells until bright pink. Stir in the carrot, leek and onion, and cook these for about 10 minutes until nicely caramelised. Stir in the Pernod and cook until it evaporates, then add the wine and cook until syrupy. Add the tomato and tomato purée. Cook for a further 5 minutes until the pan contents look quite sticky. Pour in the stock and boil until it reduces down by half. Finally, add the cream and basil leaves. Remove the pan from the heat and allow to cool, occasionally mashing the shells with a large ladle to extract as much flavour as possible. Strain through a sieve into a smaller pan ready for reheating.

3 Heat a dry heavy-based pan and sauté the girolles to draw out the moisture. Drain on kitchen paper towel, and pour away the liquid from the pan. Heat the butter in the pan and, when it stops foaming, sauté the girolles quickly until nicely cooked. Season and sprinkle with a little chopped parsley. Keep warm.

4 Cook the linguine in boiling salted water until *al dente*, 2–3 minutes. Drain and mix with a couple of spoonfuls of the sauce. Keep hot.

5 Heat another frying pan with a little oil and sauté the lobster meat for 2–3 minutes. Slice the tail meat into medallions and season.

6 Reheat the remaining sauce. Serve the linguine in the centre of four warmed plates. Place lobster and girolles on top, spoon over the sauce and sprinkle with the last of the parsley.

Poached wild salmon with Gewürztraminer sauce

Wild salmon has a leaner texture, darker colour and finer flavour than farmed salmon, purely because it grows in a totally natural ocean environment – swimming in strong currents and feeding on a completely wild diet. Yet ironically it cannot be classified as 'organic' because governing bodies cannot guarantee the origin of its feed. In season from February through to August, you will find the price reflects the prime quality. A rich fish, salmon suits sweet wine sauces, especially the spicy Alsace Gewürztraminer wine. Serve with blanched and buttery wild asparagus and an accompaniment of baby new Maris Piper potatoes and broccoli florets in an almondy-butter dressing. **SERVES 4 AS A MAIN DISH**

4 *darnes* of wild salmon (cutlets from
   the middle of the fish with a central
   bone and skin), about 150g each
Court Bouillon (page 212), for poaching
120g wild or thin asparagus spears
a little melted butter
sea salt and freshly ground black pepper

Sauce
300ml Gewürztraminer wine
300ml Fish Stock (page 212)
3 tablespoons double cream
25g butter

1 Make sure the salmon is clean and free of any blood in the cavity region. Bring the court bouillon to a gentle boil, then slip in the *darnes*. Remove from the heat and leave the fish to cook in the residual heat for 10 minutes.

2 Meanwhile, to make the sauce, boil the wine and stock together until reduced down by half to 300ml. Whisk in the cream and butter, and check the seasoning.

3 Blanch the asparagus in boiling water for 2 minutes, then drain and refresh in ice-cold water. Drain again, then place in a small saucepan with a little melted butter ready for reheating.

4 Remove the fish from the bouillon when it feels firm. Carefully pull out the central bones and gently peel away the skin. Lay the *darnes* on warmed dinner plates.

5 Briefly reheat the asparagus in the melted butter, then place over the salmon. Spoon over a little sauce and strain the rest into a sauceboat to hand round separately.

Wild salmon with wilted lettuce and cucumber salad and a vine tomato butter sauce

The wild salmon season starts in February and lasts through the summer months. These free, wild cousins of farmed salmon have a darker, less fatty flesh and a fuller flavour. Out of season, the next best salmon is that reared in Scottish lochs, on a near natural (organic) diet, with artificial currents to encourage them to develop muscle. The salad and sauce here are both Mediterranean-inspired. **SERVES 4 AS A MAIN DISH**

4 thick-cut fillets of wild salmon,
  about 150g each, skinned
3 tablespoons olive oil
1 large cucumber, peeled and diced
2 tomatoes, skinned, seeded and chopped
100g black olives, stoned and chopped
1 tablespoon chopped fresh parsley
2 baby Little Gem lettuces
3 tablespoons Classic Vinaigrette (page 213)
sea salt and freshly ground black pepper

Sauce
250g vine-ripened tomatoes
1 teaspoon sherry vinegar
1 teaspoon caster sugar
1 tablespoon chopped fresh basil
100ml double cream
50g butter, diced

1 Rub both sides of the fillets with 1 tablespoon of the olive oil and set aside.

2 Mix together the cucumber, tomatoes, olives and parsley. Season well and set this salad aside.

3 Make the sauce: halve the tomatoes and whiz with the vinegar, sugar and basil in a food processor. Pour through a sieve into a saucepan, rubbing with the back of a ladle. Cook, uncovered, for about 10 minutes until reduced by half. Mix in the cream and simmer for a minute or two, then whisk in the diced butter until nice and smooth. Season and set aside.

4 Divide the lettuces into leaves, discarding the core. Heat the remaining oil and sauté the leaves for about 2 minutes until wilted. Season and set aside.

5 Heat a heavy-based non-stick frying pan and, when hot, add the salmon, skinned side down. Turn the heat to medium and cook for 3–4 minutes. Season the fish as it cooks. Turn over carefully and cook the other side for 2–3 minutes until the fish feels lightly springy. Season again.

6 To serve, dress the salad with the vinaigrette and place in the centre of four dinner plates. (In the restaurant we mould it neatly in a plain scone cutter.) Arrange the wilted lettuce on top and then the salmon. Serve the sauce around.

Wild brown trout with a lemon and caviar sabayon

I adore fishing, and sneak out to beaches or river banks whenever I can. From May to August is the mayfly season, so I head down to the river Kennet near Hungerford and cast my line with a mayfly bait (sprayed with oil to help it float). When I land brown trout, this is how I like to cook and serve them at home, with a classically simple light and eggy sabayon flavoured with lemon and a spoon of Osietra caviar. Baby new potatoes and fresh peas are the best accompaniments.

SERVES 4 AS A MAIN DISH

2 wild brown trout, about 1kg each
2 large globe artichokes
a squeeze of lemon juice
a little olive oil, for frying
a good knob of butter
sea salt and freshly ground black pepper

Sabayon
6 free-range egg yolks
1 teaspoon lemon juice
grated zest of 1 small lemon
1 tablespoon Osietra caviar

1 Fillet the trouts, leaving the skin on. (Or ask your fishmonger to do this.) Check the flesh for pinbones with your fingertips and pull out with tweezers or thin pliers. Score the skin several times in even cuts using the tip of a razor-sharp knife. Set aside.

2 Cut off the artichoke stalks, pull off the leaves and cut out the hairy choke, to leave the hearts. (See photographs of this technique on page 216.) Cook the hearts in boiling salted water with a good squeeze of lemon juice for about 15 minutes. Drain and cool, then cut into diamonds or slices.

3 Fry the pieces of artichoke heart in a little oil and butter until nicely browned. Drain and keep warm.

4 Preheat the grill. Meanwhile, make the sabayon. Whisk the yolks, lemon juice, 1 tablespoon water and seasoning in a bowl set over a pan of simmering water until the mixture triples in volume and becomes light and frothy. (Best to do this with a hand-held electric mixer.) Remove the bowl from the water and set aside whilst you cook the trout.

5 Brush the trout skin with a little oil and grill for about 4 minutes to crisp the skin. Turn over, season the flesh and brush with more oil. Return to the grill and cook for a few more minutes until just browned. Reduce the heat to low and continue cooking until the trout feels just firm but still springy when pressed, 4–5 more minutes.

6 Return the bowl of sabayon to the simmering water and whisk quickly to froth up. Then off the heat fold in the lemon zest and caviar.

7 Dish the fish onto four warmed plates, arrange the artichoke pieces around and spoon the sauce over the top. Serve immediately.

Turbot with courgette flower fritters and Noilly Prat sauce

When courgette flowers are in season, I like to dip them in a light beer batter and fry them, holding them down with a spatula in the hot oil so they cook flat. These go on top of fillets of turbot, served on a bed of wilted spinach with a Noilly Prat velouté. **SERVES 4 AS A MAIN DISH**

4 courgette flowers, still with
   tiny whole courgettes attached
120ml tepid milk
75g plain flour, plus extra for dusting
1 teaspoon easy-blend dried yeast
1 teaspoon beer
1 medium courgette, cut into small even dice
light olive oil, for frying
4 fillets of turbot, about 125g each,
   skinned (ideally cut in *tranche* shapes)
15g butter
250ml Fish Stock (page 212)
120g baby leaf spinach

Sauce
2 shallots, chopped
10g butter
100ml dry white wine
120ml Noilly Prat
250ml Fish Stock (page 212)
1 teaspoon chopped fresh tarragon
200ml double cream
a squeeze of lemon juice
sea salt and freshly ground black
   pepper

1 First, make the sauce. Sauté the shallots in the butter for 5 minutes until softened. Pour in the wine and Noilly Prat and cook until reduced to a syrupy consistency. Add the fish stock and tarragon. Boil until reduced by half. Add the cream and boil until reduced by half again. Check the seasoning, add a squeeze of lemon juice and pass through a sieve into a clean pan. Set aside.

2 Now, for the flowers. Split the tiny courgettes (still attached to the flowers) up the middle. Whisk the milk with the flour, yeast, beer and a good pinch of salt. Set aside.

3 Lightly sauté the diced courgette in a little hot oil until lightly coloured. Season and drain on kitchen paper towel. Preheat the oven to 200°C, Gas 6.

4 Heat a tablespoon of oil in a non-stick frying pan (with an ovenproof handle) and, when hot, fry the turbot until it caramelises nicely on one side. Slide in the butter and carefully flip the fish over. Pour in the fish stock. Cover with a butter paper and transfer to the oven to cook for about 7 minutes, basting once with the stock. Remove the fish and allow to stand.

5 Now back to the courgette flowers. Toss them with a little flour. Heat 2cm depth of oil in a deep frying pan to about 180°C. When it is hot, dip a flower into the batter, press open the tiny courgette and slip it gently into the hot oil. Using a spatula, hold the courgette open if possible so it cooks flat. Cook for a minute or two until golden brown, then remove and drain. Repeat with the other flowers.

6 To serve, make sure your plates are very hot, and press the spinach leaves into the centre of each, so they wilt. Drain the turbot and put a fillet on each mound of spinach. Reheat the diced courgette in a small pan and sprinkle over. Reheat the sauce and nappé the fish with a little; serve the rest separately in a little jug. Finally, top the fish with the courgette flowers.

Fricassée of scallops and girolles with lettuce sauce

Girolles, the little, golden fairy-like mushrooms with a divine flavour, are one of the culinary delights of summer. They need to be peeled at the stalk end, but after that is done this is quite a quick dish to put together. (Out of season, you may like to use dried girolles, which can be restored by soaking and then patting dry.) Make sure the scallops you use are plump king scallops – mine are hand-dived in cold Scottish waters. The sauce is unusual, a light cream of lettuce. In the restaurant we also garnish this with whole garlic cloves confit in goose fat until the skins become crispy. An ideal dish served as a light summery lunch. **SERVES 4 AS A LIGHT DISH OR 6 AS A STARTER**

300g small summer girolles
1 large Little Gem or small Cos
  lettuce, shredded
1 clove garlic, peeled and left whole
50g smoked lean bacon, chopped
4 spring onions, chopped
4–6 tablespoons olive oil
100ml Classic Vinaigrette (page 213)
juice of ½ small lemon

1 tablespoon chopped fresh chives,
  plus extra for sprinkling
1 tablespoon chopped fresh chervil,
  plus extra sprigs to garnish
6 large fresh scallops, removed
  from their shells, without corals
½ teaspoon mild curry powder
sea salt and freshly ground black pepper

1 Using a small sharp knife, trim the ends of the girolles. Set aside.

2 Make the sauce. Sauté the lettuce with the garlic clove, bacon and one of the spring onions in 1 tablespoon of the oil until wilted, 3–5 minutes. Remove the garlic clove and discard. Whiz the lettuce, bacon and onion plus any pan juices in a food processor, then pass through a sieve into another small pan, rubbing with the back of a ladle. Season, return the sauce to a simmer and cook for 3 minutes to reduce down by about a third. Beat in the vinaigrette and set aside.

3 Heat a frying pan with 2 tablespoons of the oil and sauté the girolles and the rest of the spring onions with the lemon juice, stirring occasionally, for about 3 minutes. Season and mix in the chopped herbs. Set aside and keep warm.

4 When you are ready to serve, heat the last of the oil in a frying pan. Add the scallops, arranging them in a circle. Season nicely and sprinkle over the curry powder. After 2 minutes, turn the scallops, in the same order you placed them in the pan, and cook the other side until nicely golden, 1–2 minutes. Season again. The scallops should feel quite bouncy when pressed lightly. Don't overcook them. Slice each in half horizontally.

5 To serve, spoon the girolle mixture in the centre of four warmed plates and arrange the scallops on top. Spoon the sauce around and finish with a sprinkling of chives and a sprig of chervil.

Roasted sea bass with chive crème fraîche, baby potatoes and artichokes

This dish is so simple and so fresh. Wild sea bass, reared and caught naturally, has a greater depth of flavour than farmed. It also has a firmer texture because the fish swim against tides and currents and so develop leaner muscle. Match it with other summer favourites – firm waxy new potatoes and fresh artichoke hearts or crisp green beans. SERVES 4 AS A MAIN DISH

2 large globe artichokes
1 tablespoon lemon juice
500g new potatoes (such as
   Jersey Royals)
2 tablespoons chopped fresh chives
100g thick crème fraîche
6 tablespoons olive oil
1 tablespoon shredded fresh basil
100ml Classic Vinaigrette (page 213)
2 shallots, finely chopped

1 tablespoon sherry vinegar
2 tablespoons double cream
800g fillet of sea bass, trimmed
   and cut into 4 neat portions, skin on
sprigs fresh thyme, to garnish
sea salt and freshly ground black pepper

1 Cut off the artichoke stalks, pull off the leaves and cut out the hairy choke, leaving you with just the cup-shaped meaty hearts (see photographs of this technique on page 216). Cut the hearts into lengths and then into diamond shapes.

2 Cook the pieces of artichoke in boiling water with the lemon juice for 10 minutes until barely tender; drain. At the same time, boil the new potatoes in another pan until only just tender; drain when they are ready, then cut them in half.

3 Meanwhile, mix the chives into the crème fraîche and season nicely. Set aside.

4 Heat 2 tablespoons of the oil in a frying pan and sauté the potatoes for about 5 minutes until nicely coloured. Remove with a slotted spoon and drain on kitchen paper towel. Beat the basil into the vinaigrette, then mix with the warm potatoes and leave to cool.

5 Add the artichokes to the frying pan, with another tablespoon of oil if necessary, and sauté for 3–5 minutes until nicely coloured. Remove with a slotted spoon, drain and keep warm.

6 Add the shallots to the pan and sauté for 5 minutes until softened. Deglaze with the vinegar and cook until the liquid has reduced away. Stir in the cream, season and set aside to keep warm.

7 Score the skin of the bass several times with the tip of a very sharp knife. Heat the remaining oil in a large frying pan. Season the bass and cook, skin side down, for 3–4 minutes until the silver skin is crispy. Turn carefully and cook the other side for 1–2 minutes until lightly springy when pressed. Season again.

8 To serve, spoon the artichokes in the centre of four warmed plates. Spoon the shallot cream on top. Sit the sea bass on this, arrange the basil potatoes around the fish and garnish with thyme. Finally, spoon the chive crème fraîche on top so it melts invitingly over the fish as you serve.

Sautéed foie gras with peach chutney

This is the ultimate quick snack, once you've made the chutney. Foie gras needs to be fresh – order it from a reputable butcher, such as one that belongs to the exclusive 'Q' Guild. Follow the instructions carefully for preparing and cooking it, as it is too special to mess up. French chef Michel Bras has a good trick: he freezes fresh foie gras first, so it doesn't overcook on the outside and render away too much fat. To do this, cut the foie gras in slices and freeze, interleaved with freezer tissue. If you like, serve the foie gras on thinly sliced fresh peach.

SERVES 6 AS A LIGHT DISH OR STARTER

100ml balsamic vinegar
1 lobe fresh foie gras, about 400g
sea salt and freshly ground black pepper

To serve
Peach Chutney (page 213)
slices of hot brioche toast

1 Boil the balsamic vinegar to reduce it by half, then set aside to cool whilst you prepare the foie gras.

2 Fresh foie gras is easily damaged, so handle it with care. Let it soften for 20 minutes at room temperature so you can prise it apart gently without it breaking. There are two unequal halves connected by a thick blood vessel that runs across both sides. Using a table knife, work your way through the soft rich flesh, carefully pulling the tube away. You may find it useful to have a thin pair of scissors handy to snip into awkward areas. Don't worry too much if you break bits off accidentally, as you can reshape these inside the lobe, but try to keep it as intact as possible. Also don't worry about smaller veins – these dissolve on cooking. Cut the foie gras into six slices.

3 Heat a non-stick frying pan and, when you can feel a good heat rising, add the slices of foie gras – no need for any oil, as there is enough fat in the livers already. Season during cooking. Cook for about a minute on each side. Do not overcook – the slices will carry on cooking a little whilst they are resting out of the pan. The outside should be deliciously caramelised and the insides still pink and creamy.

4 Serve with the pan juices poured over and the balsamic vinegar trickled around. Accompany with peach chutney and brioche toast.

Ribeye of beef with watercress purée

Ribeye is very much a Scottish cut of beef, which more chefs are beginning to use. It comes from the top end of the sirloin, is a nice round shape, cooks well and – more important – has a great flavour and texture. We buy it in 2-kilo pieces and 'set' the shape by rolling it tightly into a ballotine and storing it in the fridge for 2 days. It can then be cut into thick steaks and grilled or pan-fried. We serve ribeye with an eye-catching watercress purée that is embarrassingly simple to make. (In the restaurant we wring out the watercress purée in a cloth and serve it as a soft quenelle, but if you prefer a pouring sauce then use the maximum amount of cream.) Sit the steaks on a bed of sautéed mushrooms of your choice. I prefer girolles, but you can use ceps, oysters or even the brown champignons de Paris. **SERVES 4 AS A MAIN DISH**

600g piece ribeye of beef
3 tablespoons olive oil
15g butter
200g mushrooms (see above), sliced if large
2 fat cloves garlic, finely chopped
2 teaspoons chopped fresh parsley
sea salt and freshly ground black pepper

Sauce
300g watercress
100g spinach leaves
60–200ml double cream

1 First, make the sauce. Put a pan of salted water on to boil. Push in all the watercress and boil for 5 minutes. Add the spinach and cook for another minute or so until wilted. Drain in a colander. Press with the back of a ladle to extract as much moisture as possible.

2 Put the leaves into a food processor and whiz to a fine purée, scraping down the sides occasionally. Pour 60ml of the cream through the processor funnel and keep the blades whirling for what seems like an eternity. You will eventually get a sauce with a texture like silk. It will be so smooth, you will not need to pass it through a sieve. If you want a pouring sauce, add the remaining cream. Check the seasoning, and pour into a small saucepan ready for reheating.

3 Cut the ribeye into 4 even steaks and rub each side using 1 tablespoon oil. Heat a heavy non-stick frying pan until you can feel a good heat rising. Lay in your steaks – they should give a good hiss as they hit the hot pan. Season the tops and cook for about 3 minutes, then flip over and cook the other side for 2 minutes. Slip the butter into the pan at this stage and season the second side. Remove the steaks from the pan and leave to rest while you cook the mushrooms.

4 Sauté the mushrooms with the garlic in the remaining oil. Season and mix with the parsley.

5 Reheat the watercress purée/sauce. Place the steaks on warmed plates (sliced first if you like), trickle over any pan juices and spoon on the mushrooms. If your watercress purée is firm, shape it into quenelles. If it is a sauce, spoon some over the steaks and hand round the rest separately. Serve with whatever accompaniment you like to eat steak with. Chips are great (see my recipe on page 197), or why not try slices of really fresh baguette?

Baked white peaches
with thyme icecream

If you dust whole fruits with icing sugar and caster sugar, and trickle with some melted butter, you will find they take on a delicious colour and sweet chargrilled flavour. Add a few fresh thyme flowers during the cooking and discover a great new culinary idea: baking fruits with aromatic herbs rather than just spices. To stay in the thyme mood, I suggest a creamy thyme-flavoured icecream to accompany the peaches. **SERVES 4**

4 whole white peaches, ripe
   but not overripe and not bruised
50g icing sugar
50g caster sugar
1 vanilla pod
25g unsalted butter, melted
1–2 tablespoons Cointreau
   or Grand Marnier
1 teaspoon fresh thyme leaves
   stripped from the stalks
Thyme Icecream (page 214), to serve

1 Preheat the oven to 190°C, Gas 5. Wash the peaches. Mix the two sugars together and roll the fruits in them to coat. Sit the peaches in a shallow ovenproof dish.
2 Slit open the vanilla pod, scrape out the seeds and mix into the butter. Trickle this over the peaches.
3 Bake, uncovered, for about 5 minutes, then remove and spoon over the caramelising juices that have formed in the dish. Continue baking for 10 minutes, spooning over the juices once or twice more.
4 About 5 minutes before the end of cooking, spoon over the liqueur and sprinkle over the thyme leaves so their fragrance can be absorbed by the fruits. Remove and cool until warm.
5 Serve the warm peaches with a scoop of icecream alongside.

Roasted figs with cinnamon shortbreads

Roasting fruits in a caramel sauce is a quick and easy way to cook them. I also like to spike the syrup with a splash of balsamic vinegar – particularly good with fresh figs, which appear in our shops in late summer. This way of cooking also suits small pears and whole peaches. You can serve them as is, perhaps with some icecream (rich vanilla icecream is sensational), or take the time to make some melt-in-the mouth spicy shortbreads too. SERVES 4

8 fresh figs
70g icing sugar
40g unsalted butter
1 tablespoon balsamic vinegar

Shortbreads
125g unsalted butter, softened
90g caster sugar
1 large free-range egg, beaten
250g plain flour
$\frac{1}{2}$ teaspoon ground cinnamon
a good pinch of fine sea salt

1 First, make the shortbread dough. Beat the butter and sugar with an electric mixer until light and fluffy. Gradually add the beaten egg.

2 Sift together the flour, cinnamon and salt. With the machine on the lowest speed, slowly add the flour and beat until the mixture comes together in a soft dough. Scrape down the sides occasionally.

3 Scoop the dough onto a sheet of cling film and gently shape it into a roll about 5cm in diameter. Wrap and chill until firm. (The dough can be kept a good week in the fridge, or you can freeze it for up to a month, to have home-made biscuits in a thrice. Cut off discs with a serrated knife and bake from frozen.)

4 Preheat the oven to 150°C, Gas 2. Cut rounds from the firm dough roll the thickness of a £1 coin. Place on a baking sheet. Make at least 8 for this dessert. If you want biscuits with neat edges, press down on each with a pastry cutter. Don't prick them. Bake until lightly coloured, 20–25 minutes.

5 Cool for a minute or so on the baking sheet, then slide off onto a wire rack to crisp up. As they cool, you could sprinkle them with a little caster sugar, but it is not necessary.

6 For the fruit, snip the tips off the figs using scissors, then cut each in four almost to the base, so they form a petal shape. Heat the icing sugar and butter slowly in a frying pan, stirring until the sugar has dissolved, then mix in the balsamic vinegar.

7 Stand the figs upright in the pan and spoon over the syrup. Cook on a low heat for about 7 minutes, spooning over the syrup as the fruit softens. The figs should retain their shape. Remove from the heat and cool in the pan.

8 In the restaurant we serve a fig sitting on a biscuit. You might like to simply serve them side by side.

Cherry soup with caramel balsamic icecream

In July 1998 I was privileged to cook for the World Cup Final dinner held in the Orangery in Versailles. What a night! The planning required several trips to Paris, and on one of these I visited a restaurant where I was served a fruit soup with the most amazing icecream. It turned out to be a caramel flavour to which had been added aged balsamic vinegar. For the soup, you need deep red cherries to give not only flavour but also a rich mahogany colour. **SERVES 4**

300g dark red cherries, stoned
200ml Stock Syrup (page 214)
3–4 leaves fresh lemon balm

Icecream
250g caster sugar
3 tablespoons balsamic vinegar
6 free-range egg yolks
500ml milk
150ml double cream

1 First, make the caramel for the icecream. Put the sugar into a heavy-based saucepan and slowly heat until it starts to melt. (You might want to add a couple of tablespoons of water to help the process, and you can stir gently once or twice. True chefs, however, make caramel without water!) If you get crystals round the edge of the pan, wash them down with a pastry brush dipped in water. Stir occasionally until the crystals have all dissolved. When all the sugar has melted, slowly raise the heat and boil the sugar syrup until it starts to turn golden brown and then a mid-brown. Have ready a big bowl of iced water. As soon as the syrup is the right colour, immerse the base of the pan in the water to cool the caramel. When cool, stir in the balsamic vinegar and set aside.

2 Now make the custard for the icecream. Place the egg yolks in a bowl set on a damp cloth (which holds it steady) and whisk until pale golden. Bring the milk and cream slowly to the boil in a heavy-based saucepan. Slowly pour the creamy milk onto the yolks, whisking steadily. When it is all incorporated, tip the lot back into the saucepan and return to a low heat. Stir until the mixture just starts to thicken (it should be 82°C). Do not allow it to even start to bubble, or it may curdle. Remove and cool.

3 Make the soup. Reserve half the cherries (I'd suggest the best looking ones), and cut them in half if large. Roughly chop the rest. Bring the stock syrup to the boil and add the chopped cherries and lemon balm leaves. Remove from the heat and leave to infuse for about 15 minutes, then remove the lemon balm.

4 Whiz the fruit and syrup mixture in a food processor or blender until smooth, then pass through a sieve into a bowl, rubbing through with the back of a ladle. Chill the soup.

5 Back to the icecream. Mix the cooled caramel into the cool custard. Pour into an icecream machine and churn until icy smooth and creamy. Scoop into a rigid plastic food container and freeze until just solid.

6 When ready to serve, divide the soup among four chilled shallow bowls. Sit a scoop of icecream in the centre and drop the reserved cherries around the icecream. Serve immediately.

Wild strawberry shortcakes

As a Scot I'm partial to a nice crisp shortbread, but I prefer to make mine using a pâte sablée dough. I cut out elegant biscuits the size of a coffee saucer and press a slight dip in the centre. After baking, this is filled with a thick strawberry coulis, and dainty wild (Alpine) strawberries are arranged around the edge. Wild strawberries, originally from mountainous regions of Europe (hence the alternative name Alpine), are a different species from the common ones – their seeds stick up, whilst cultivated fruits have seeds that press into the flesh. **SERVES 6**

250g ripe strawberries, hulled
1 tablespoon caster sugar, or to taste
a squeeze of lemon juice
2 tablespoons thick double cream
about 300g wild strawberries, hulled

Shortcakes
4 large free-range egg yolks
120g caster sugar, plus extra for sprinkling
120g unsalted butter, softened
170g strong (bread) flour, plus extra
   for rolling
1¹/₂ teaspoons baking powder

1 First make the shortcake dough. Beat the egg yolks with the sugar until thick and creamy, then gradually beat in the butter. Sift the flour and baking powder together, and mix in. Knead lightly to a soft dough, then wrap in cling film and chill for 30 minutes.

2 On a lightly floured board, roll out the dough to a thickness of 5mm. Cut out 6 discs about 12cm diameter, re-rolling as necessary. Use a coffee saucer as a template. Place on a non-stick baking sheet, and prick the discs a few times with a fork. Press the centres to make a slight dip and, if you like, pinch the edges into a slight rim. Chill for 30 minutes.

3 Preheat the oven to 150°C, Gas 2. Sprinkle the discs with a little sugar and bake for 12 minutes or until pale golden. Allow to sit on the baking sheet for a minute to firm, then, using a palette knife to help, slide onto a wire rack to cool and crisp.

4 Process the large strawberries to a purée, adding sugar to taste plus a squeeze of lemon juice and the double cream.

5 Just before serving, spoon the strawberry coulis into the centre of the shortbreads, and arrange wild strawberries around the side. Serve with sweetened, lightly whipped cream.

Pannacotta with raspberries

Scottish raspberries, in season during July and August, are a blissful match for this pannacotta, which is simple and sublime. I have Hilary Brown, a fellow Scot, to thank for the recipe. When homegrown raspberries are out of season, try slices of ripe star fruit soaked in a grenadine-flavoured syrup. Buy liquid glucose from a chemist and measure it as you would honey, that is spooning it out of the jar with a hot metal spoon. **SERVES 6–8**

300g caster sugar
4 tablespoons liquid glucose
600ml double cream
150ml milk
3 leaves gelatine
2 tablespoons rum
300–400g fresh raspberries

1 First, make the caramel. Put 150g of the sugar into a heavy-based saucepan with the glucose (this keeps the caramel viscous when cool) and 50ml water. Place over a low heat and stir occasionally until the liquid no longer feels gritty. Make sure there are no sugar grains clinging to the sides of the pan either. Meanwhile, fill a basin with iced water.

2 Raise the heat and allow the syrup to bubble until it reaches a nice caramel colour, 175°C on a sugar thermometer. Do not stir the syrup at all whilst it is bubbling. As soon as the caramel is ready, remove it from the heat and lower the base of the pan carefully into the iced water. Hold the pan there for a minute or two until the temperature drops. This stops the syrup continuing to cook and burning. Remove from the water and set aside to cool a bit.

3 Now make the cream. Put the cream and milk into a large saucepan and bring slowly to the boil. When the liquid starts to creep up the sides of the pan, adjust the heat so it maintains a medium boil, and hold it at this for a good 5 minutes so the liquid reduces down a little.

4 Meanwhile, put the gelatine leaves into a bowl of cold water to soak for a few minutes until they soften, then drain off all the water.

5 Stir the remaining sugar and the rum into the boiling cream and allow to dissolve. Remove from the heat and cool for a few seconds, then slip in the softened gelatine and stir well until dissolved. Set aside to cool.

6 Place 6–8 dariole moulds of 120ml capacity on a tray. Spoon about 2 teaspoons of the warm caramel into each. Slowly pour in the cream, right up to the top. Chill until set.

7 To serve, dip the dariole moulds in hot water for a few seconds, then pull the set cream away from the sides of the mould. Invert and shake out onto individual dessert plates. (Wet these first with cold water, so you can slide the pannacotta into position should it come out offside, then wipe the moisture off with kitchen paper towel.) Arrange raspberries around each pannacotta and trickle over any leftover caramel.

Fruit salad in a glass

For this you need a glorious selection of fresh fruits from the summer harvest. Lemon balm grows well in town and country gardens, or you can buy sprigs from speciality greengrocers. Alternatively, use fresh mint with a touch of fresh lemon zest. Serve in tall elegant glasses with a spoonful of shaved Champagne sherbet on top. Champagne is the wine I use for this refreshing ice, but any good dry sparkling white wine, such as those from New Zealand or Australia, would do. Or try it with pink Champagne. The texture is light and crunchy, like an Italian granita. **SERVES 4**

2 Granny Smith apples

2 ripe pears (Comice, Packham
  or small Conference)

1 ripe yellow peach

1 large orange

100ml Stock Syrup (page 214)

juice of 1 small lemon

1 large star fruit

5 sprigs fresh lemon balm

250g mixed fresh summer berries
  (such as strawberries, raspberries
  and red or white currants)

Champagne sherbet

200g caster sugar

3 tablespoons liquid glucose

½ x 75cl bottle Champagne

To decorate (optional)

sugared coriander leaf
  (page 205)

1 First, make the sherbet. Dissolve the sugar in 175ml water over a gentle heat, stirring occasionally. Add the glucose. Simmer for 5 minutes, then pour in the Champagne and remove at once from the heat. Allow to cool, then pour into a shallow freezerproof container and chill. When cold, freeze until partially frozen.

2 Remove and whisk with a strong metal fork so the crystals are broken up to a slush. Re-freeze lightly again, then repeat the whisking to make a gritty texture. Seal the container and store in the freezer until required. (This makes about 750ml of sherbet.)

3 Core the apples and pears, then slice thinly (no need to peel). Peel, stone and slice the peach. Peel and segment the orange. Toss the prepared fruit with the stock syrup and lemon juice in a bowl. Slice the star fruit and mix into the bowl along with the lemon balm. Leave to infuse for about 15 minutes, then discard the lemon balm.

4 About 10 minutes before serving, remove the sherbet from the freezer and let it soften at room temperature.

5 Hull the strawberries and cut in half. Remove the stalks from currants, if using. Mix the berries gently into the fruit salad.

6 Spoon the fruit salad into four tall wine glasses, and top with any leftover syrup. Scrape the sherbet out of the freezer container with a metal spoon so you obtain slushy shavings, like snow, and spoon them on top of each glass. Serve immediately.

Mille-feuille of chocolate with lavender

Lavender is a herb we normally associate with bathing, not baking. But in the parts of Europe where it grows in profusion (Provence in France and also nearer home in Norfolk), it is often sprinkled into bread doughs and sweet baking. I steep a spoonful of dried lavender heads in a light chocolate ganache, which I pipe between thin, crisp puff pastry wafers. I continue the floral fragrance by serving this with scoops of lavender icecream (follow the recipe for Thyme Icecream on page 214, substituting a dessertspoon of dried lavender flowers for the sprigs of thyme).

SERVES 4

about 300g home-made Puff Pastry (page 214)
  or 1 x 375g pack ready-rolled puff pastry
200ml Crème Anglaise (page 214)
1 dessertspoon dried lavender flowers
300g dark chocolate with 60% cocoa solids
  (we use Valrhona), broken in small chunks
200ml double cream

To finish
cocoa powder

1 Roll out the pastry to a rectangle slightly larger than 30 x 40cm, which will allow enough excess so you can trim the edges neatly. (It is important to get even shapes for serving.) Cut into four long rectangles of 30 x 10cm. Using a long palette knife, lift these onto a baking sheet and score each across into four equal rectangles. Chill for 20 minutes whilst you preheat the oven to 200°C, Gas 6.

2 Bake for 10 minutes, then place another heavy baking sheet on top of the pastry rectangles (this helps to keep them flat). Bake for another 10–12 minutes until golden brown and crisp. Remove and cool on a wire rack.

3 Now for the cream. Warm the crème anglaise gently and stir in the lavender flowers. Leave to steep off the heat for 30 minutes, then strain and discard the flowers.

4 Return the crème anglaise to a gentle heat to warm again, then remove and stir in the chocolate. Leave until melted, then whisk until shiny. Set aside to cool.

5 Whip the double cream until it is softly stiff. Fold into the chocolate mixture.

6 Make four layered 'sandwiches' with the pastry rectangles and chocolate cream, either spreading or piping the cream in between the pastry layers. Dust the top with cocoa powder. Serve with small scoops or quenelles of lavender or vanilla icecream.

Jasmine custards

If you are looking for a variation on the crème brûlée theme, try this. Jasmine is in flower anytime from midsummer through to early autumn, depending on the position of the bush in the garden. I've seen jasmine in flower in June and in early October, hanging over various town gardens around my part of London. You'll need a large mugful of the delicate white flowers for this recipe. Incidentally, if you are given a potted jasmine plant as a present for indoors, when it has finished flowering, plant it against a sunny wall or fence in the garden. Within a year or two you'll have a good supply of flowers. **SERVES 6**

375ml double cream
200ml creamy milk
50g fresh jasmine flowers
6 large free-range egg yolks
70g caster sugar
some demerara sugar, to caramelise (optional)

1 Heat the cream and milk in a saucepan and allow the liquid to rise up the sides of the pan before removing from the heat. Stir in the jasmine flowers and leave until cold.
2 Strain into a clean heavy-based pan, pressing the flowers in the sieve with the back of a ladle to extract the fragrance.
3 Preheat the oven to 140°C, Gas 1. Reheat the cream. Meanwhile, beat the egg yolks in a large bowl set on a damp cloth to keep it steady. When the cream starts to creep up the sides of the pan again, pour a small amount onto the yolks and whisk to blend. Keep whisking in the hot liquid, in cautious amounts so it doesn't curdle.
4 Strain the mixture back into the pan and stir in the caster sugar. Heat on the lowest possible setting, stirring frequently, until the custard coats the back of the spoon. Pour into six elegant heatproof containers such as ramekins or pretty heatproof teacups.
5 Bake the custards for 45–60 minutes until the sides come away from the edge of the container when tipped slightly. The centre should remain slightly wobbly. Remove from the oven and cool, then chill until set.
6 If you like, you can sprinkle some demerara sugar in an even layer on top and caramelise this with a blow torch before serving.

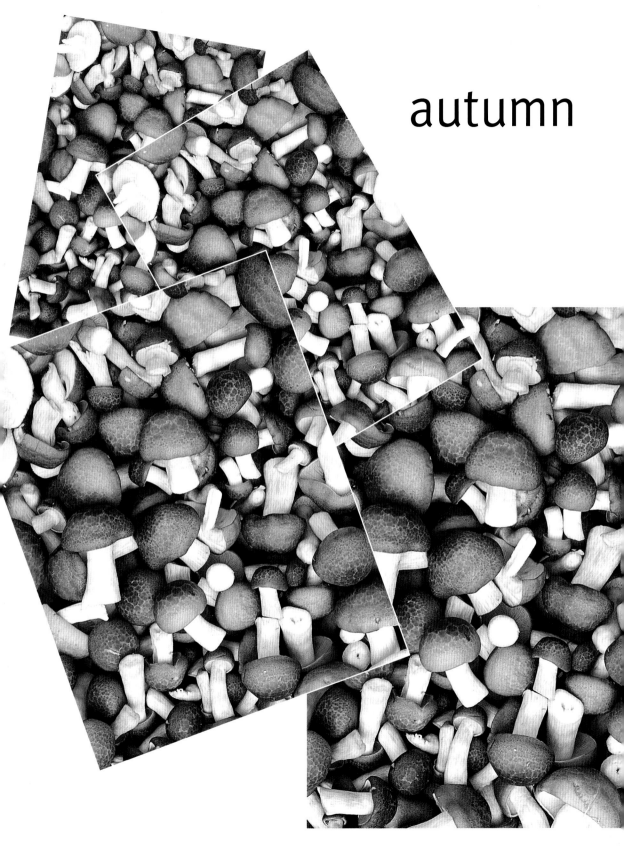

autumn

Our British summers are 'variable', but then I don't enjoy too much summer heat. In fact, when the days begin to shorten and we wake to an autumnal nip in the air, I do feel a tinge of relief. And excitement too, because with autumn comes the promise of bountiful harvests of fruits and vegetables at their best.

Of all the leafy vegetables that pass through my kitchen, I suppose **sorrel** is one of the most tricky to handle. The peppery astringent taste is terrific in lifting the flavour of fish dishes (especially poached salmon), soups and salads, but knowing when to add it is the key to success. If added too soon, the leaves wilt to a slimy dull green, so it is best to put it in at the last minute. Cooks sometimes add a handful of baby spinach leaves to a sorrel dish to enhance the colour, but I find this unnecessary if you leave it until the last moment. If you grow sorrel, pick the leaves just before you need them. The ideal size for flavour is about the length of a large bay leaf. Peel the fine fibres from the stalk, then shred the leaves. They are delicate and bruise easily, even more so than basil, so always use the sharpest knife you can.

I'm really fortunate in having had a number of proud moments in my career. One of the highlights of the summer of 1999 was cooking a celebration lunch for the opening of the Scottish Parliament at Kincardine House. But there was another memorable event that day. It was my first taste of spanking fresh **spinach** picked barely a few minutes before and brought into the kitchen by the gardener himself. Where would we be now without spinach in the kitchen? Modern market gardening and transport have made this wonderful vegetable indispensable. But like sorrel, it must not be overcooked and is best added at the last minute. In the autumn, spinach leaves are larger but still wonderfully tender, and they can be used for creamed soups and for serving under medallions of fish or pink meat. Blanch the leaves for a few seconds in boiling water, then immediately drain and refresh in a bowl of iced water. Press out the excess water, then reheat at the last minute with a knob of butter.

The last decade or so has seen the popularising of many vegetables that can now be easily grown under cover, including many exotics. One of the nicest is the ragged-leaf **wild rocket**, which to the untrained eye looks like a weed. More peppery and textured than the smoother, dark green rocket, wild rocket has a lot more uses than being tossed in a salad or used as a rustic garnish. The flavour is brilliant with full-flavoured cheeses such as Parmesan and tangy goat's cheese. Mixed with fresh goat's cheese and vinaigrette it makes a wonderful filling for home-made ravioli. I also like it roughly chopped and tossed into risottos at the last moment.

No offence, but **celeriac** must be the ugliest vegetable around. Maybe that's why it is so underrated. I suppose it could be described as the Cyrano de Bergerac of the kitchen – ugly on the outside, but wonderful within. It's delicious as a purée, brilliant in soups, good deep-fried as vegetable chips or grated raw as a salad, and perfect cooked fondant-style (sautéed first and then simmered in stock). In the autumn I like a truly decadent treat of creamed celeriac topped with shavings of Périgord truffle. Sometimes as an *amuse-gueule*, we serve a tiny salad of shaved apple and celeriac bound in truffle vinaigrette. Celeriac is so versatile a vegetable, I really do enjoy cooking with it.

Looking a lot like chubby grubs, **crosnes** (see photograph on page 112) look and taste like a cross between globe artichokes and salsify, although they are completely unrelated. They were imported to France from China in the nineteenth century and grown in a village called Crosnes, from which they took their name (they're also called Chinese or Japanese artichokes). We treat them in a similar way to Jerusalem artichokes – cooked and then tossed in brown butter with chopped parsley and lemon juice. They're terrific with pigeon and with full-flavoured fish.

A truly versatile vegetable, **cauliflower** is good whatever way you want to use it. It does, however, have a downside, which is the smell if you overcook it even by a few minutes. I think that is what puts some people off eating it. My hint to lessen the smell (apart from watch the clock) is to simmer the florets in a mixture of water and milk. In the restaurant, we use only the actual florets, without any stalk, although at home you might like to trim them longer. Cauliflower is tremendous with fish, especially sweet scallops. We have one recipe where baby-size florets are dipped in a *beignet* batter

and fried as fritters. We also slice large florets thinly, season them with curry spices, salt and pepper, and then fry them in olive oil until beautifully caramelised. When cooled to room temperature, we serve them with a simple dressing of puréed raisins, capers and water.

Another vegetable we put on for our autumn menus is **fennel**. I prefer to use baby fennel – the little hearts look like crab claws and, appropriately, are brilliant served with all kinds of fish dishes. I like the baby vegetables because they are very tender yet still possess a full aniseed flavour. Older fennel bulbs need to be peeled of the stringy outside fibres. Fennel is a popular Mediterranean vegetable, especially in the South of France. In Tunisia and Morocco you see carts piled high with crisp fennel bulbs, to be served no doubt alongside spicy lamb dishes and chargrilled chicken and fish. We like to top and tail baby fennel bulbs, then cook them whole in olive oil until lightly coloured.

The **aubergine** holds a special place in my heart. A few days before opening my first restaurant in Park Walk, London, we still hadn't thought of a name, or rather agreed on one. In a flash it came to me – the Aubergine, and so it came to pass. You can stuff aubergines, cube and stew them, even fry thinly as crisps, and use in almost anything from canapés to main courses. And this vegetable can get a cook out of trouble when faced with having to prepare a hearty dish for non-meat eaters. The only thing you cannot do is eat aubergines raw. If you intend roasting, stewing or grilling them, they do not need to be salted first (we call this dégorging), but if you want to fry them, it is best to draw out excess moisture first.

Sprinkle lightly with fine sea salt and drain in a colander for 20 minutes. Then rinse well and pat dry.

Aubergines can absorb a lot of oil, if you let them. To avoid this, I toss them first in oil, then brown them in a stinking hot, dry pan. To make a creamy purée, we halve the aubergines, slash the flesh a few times, brush both sides with olive oil, season and sandwich back together with slivers of garlic and sprigs of fresh rosemary inside. Wrapped in foil and baked in a hot oven, they take about 40 minutes for the flesh to soften enough to scoop out and purée. But we haven't finished yet. The purée is heated in a dry frying pan until reduced down a little, to drive off excess moisture, then it is mixed with finely chopped tomatoes, fresh coriander, extra virgin olive oil and seasoning, to make a sublime aubergine caviar – the basis for many of my early hallmark dishes.

One of my most fraught moments during the preparation of the World Cup Dinner for over 700 people in July 1998, at Versailles in Paris, was the preparation of a garnish of deep-fried courgette leaves. These had to be dipped in a light batter, fried and then pressed between two sheets of paper to flatten. I'm happy to say that we did manage to produce delicate, gossamer-thin leaves that looked fantastic. And this does nicely illustrate how versatile the **courgette** is as a food plant. In the early autumn it is at its best, and you can use the flowers, leaves and, of course, the gourd itself as a vegetable. Courgettes contain a lot of water, so suit light cooking. We never boil them, preferring to slice them thinly and then sauté in a little olive oil, or souse in a vinaigrette. And, of course, they're a classic partner for aubergines in ratatouille. Try this idea for a starter, following the recipe for Tomato and Parmesan Gratinée Tarts on page 133, substituting courgettes for the tomatoes. After baking the pastry bases, spread with a little tapenade and arrange thinly sliced, sautéed courgettes over this. Top each tart with a thin slice of seared fresh tuna.

Perhaps because the UK is an island (and proud of it), we sometimes close our minds to foods that we think of as a bit 'foreign'. One of these is **pumpkin** – for a long time we have only associated it with Hallowe'en. Our shops have pumpkins in stock for about a fortnight at the end of October and then bang, they disappear almost overnight. What do people do with all that lovely flesh they've scraped out when making the jack o'lanterns, I wonder? Slowly, we are realising just how versatile pumpkin is, and the fact that there are several varieties. In the restaurant we like to use the pale green pumpkin with ridges, popular in France and with West Indian cooks. You don't have to buy a whole one, just a wedge or two will do nicely. And far from being in season just for a few weeks, you'll find pumpkins on sale in markets during the autumn and well into winter. We make a smooth golden soup with pumpkin, served with spicy fried scallops, and also use it as a ravioli filling. To thicken the flesh for the filling, after cooking we put it in a jelly bag and leave to drain overnight. Pumpkin makes a good simple purée to serve with rich meats such as venison or game, and 'marries' well with smoky pancetta and punchy Parmesan cheese. It has its sweet uses too. I love pumpkin with the Italian *mostarda di fruta*, and in a pumpkin and frangipane flan, which I ate when I was a young chef in Paris.

No piece on autumn foods could appear without a good discourse on wild mushrooms. We always look forward to the boxes of fascinating fungi our suppliers bring in at this time of year. The tiny Smartie-size **mousserons** (see photograph on page 104) may look dainty, but they pack a lot of flavour. Unfortunately, they are quite fiddly to clean. We use them in soups, especially with mussels, and also serve them along with globe artichokes as a garnish vegetable for veal and pigeon. Another favourite is **ceps** – sometimes as much as 10 kilos a day of fresh ceps will pass through the kitchen, to be sautéed, confit, roasted or packed in jars with olive oil. We even hang them to dry until brittle, then grind them to a fine powder to scatter over risottos and fillets of sea bass or use as a flavouring for a clear consommé. Possibly the ugliest wild mushrooms, **trompettes des morts** look dark and sinister, but I love to serve them in warm salads or with roasted fillets of turbot. Occasionally, when we can get them, we put **blewits** on the menu. I call them the acid-house mushroom, because they look like drop-outs from a rave party. Their flesh is quite bitter, so we counter this by making sure they are well and truly sautéed, even to the point of overcooking. Then we stir in a spoonful of confit of sweet shallots to temper the flavour.

I associate **mussels** with my first serious telling-off as a young chef in Paris. You see, in French restaurants, the hygiene regulations regarding mussels are very strict, and each chef who opens up a sack must pin the identifying tag to a

makes them very frisky by the time we receive them. If you flick their tails they snap straight back, certainly a sign of being very much alive. We find they peel easier if blanched for 25 seconds in boiling water, dropping just a dozen at a time into the water. Then, after peeling, we stack them in tight rows on trays and chill to firm the flesh. Their heads are full of flavour, so we sauté them to use in a langoustine stock for sauces. The heads also contain a membrane that acts as a clarifying agent for stocks, just like the albumen in egg whites – after simmering we find the liquid has become naturally clear. Langoustines are popular as ravioli fillings, or sautéed to serve with salads or in soups. We often dust them with curry powder or crushed saffron before roasting, and, for a really strong colour, sometimes dip them into green lobster coral, which cooks to a vibrant pink.

Throughout the summer and autumn months, we feature **red mullet** frequently on the menu. It is obligingly good both hot and cold. Most of my red mullet ideas come from my time in the Mediterranean – like serving crispy-skinned fillets topped with a fine black olive purée (we call this a tapenade, although I omit the usual anchovies as they are too overpowering), or placing them on cous cous scented with lemon grass. And, of course, red mullet is one of the essential fish for a classic bouillabaisse. This we serve with croûtes topped with the chopped and sautéed mullet liver mixed with olive purée. We also simply pan-fry fillets or souse them in a vinaigrette.

Red mullet is a shallow water fish, and our supplies come from Brixham in Devon or from the South of France. The

board. Then, in the unlikely event of food poisoning, the source of supply can be traced back. As the young 'rosbif' from England, I knew nothing of this and threw out the tag. Fortunately, I wasn't fluent in French then (I am now), so didn't quite understand the 'finer points' of the abuse hurled at me by chef. Ouch! Two better memories of mussels in France are baking them in the shell with brioche crumbs and Gruyère cheese, and the delightful style of matching mussels with mushrooms, which the French call *terre et mer* (earth and sea).

Hardly a day goes by when we don't have **langoustines**, also called Dublin Bay prawns, on the menu. They are indispensable as a fine food and have so many uses. Our langoustines come to us from the west of Scotland. They are transported in aerated tanks, which skins are the great attraction for me, so delicate and pretty. The scales can be easily picked off with fingers (we do this inside large bin bags). To get a firmer grip when filleting, my chefs bend the fish in a slight curve before cutting down the backbone. It's a neat trick. The bones and heads make good fish stock.

For years, diced **monkfish** was passed off as 'scampi'. Now it occupies a supreme place in fish cuisine and, where once derided as tasteless and watery, it is now in danger of culinary overkill. Like cod, we are in danger of overfishing it. You see, monkfish is a deep water fish and so is difficult to farm. It takes many years for monkfish to grow to maturity, so replenishment of stocks is slow, and supply is now falling behind demand. It is the tails we eat – the heavy bony heads are discarded. (The livers are tasty and can be cooked to serve as a garnish.) There is only one central bone, or cartilage, with two fillets on each side. These have to be skinned and the grey membrane carefully removed because it can cause the flesh to curl unattractively during cooking. After filleting, we often roll the flesh tightly in cling film, to tighten and firm it. For a few months I was Pierre Koffman's head chef at Tante Claire (now the site of my restaurant), and I remember well a brilliant monkfish recipe he did – a fillet tunneled out and stuffed with a finely diced ratatouille, then wrapped in a whole flattened, scored squid to be pan-roasted. Sheer genius. He served that with a saffron-scented risotto.

Unlike monkfish, **rabbit** is not in short supply. The French and Italians have a particular fondness for it and cook it like chicken or lean tender pork, with fresh rosemary or thyme. And hip New Yorkers

are taking to it in their chic upscale eateries. We Brits still associate rabbit with flopsy bunny (or field vermin), although it is beginning to feature on some restaurant menus. We use the shoulder meat for stews (*pot au feu*), terrines and pâtés, and roast the saddles and legs. The carcasses make good stock, which can then be used to make a setting-strength aspic jelly for pâtés *en gelée*. The legs and shoulders we also confit slowly in goose fat until the tender meat can be pulled into shreds and then mix it with vinaigrette. Rabbit is good with gnocchi and a light and creamy mustard sauce, and with a caramelised tart of chicory. And the best end can be served as tiny chops with the kidneys as a garnish.

Autumn is the time for game birds. The shooting seasons start in late summer, although some, such as pigeon, are on sale year round. I had my first hunting experience with Marco Pierre White. His aim was much surer than mine – not only did he bag his birds in flight, but also the ones I missed. But I'll learn… We get many of our game birds from the Petworth Estate in West Sussex – pheasants, wild ducks, woodcocks and so on. We get **pigeons** in from Anjou where they are reared in the wild. Most of the time we use only the breasts of wild birds, although the legs can be carved off too. The carcasses make good stock. The breasts are nice served sliced in a warm salad, and we use them as part of a game terrine such as the Mosaic of Autumn Game on page 130. Pigeon breasts are particularly delicious served with a soft swede purée and the little artichoke-flavoured crosnes. We often pan-fry **pheasant** breasts with fresh thyme or serve with a salad of apple and celeriac

tossed with a walnut vinaigrette. Older birds are used in a fricassée with lentils. If the birds have been badly shot, we use the meat to make a sausage bound with foie gras. Little dark-fleshed **wild ducks,** or sarcelles, taste like a cross between woodcock and grouse, and a lot gamier than normal ducks. Their legs are tough and sinewy, so we use a part poaching, part grilling method of cooking. Because the breasts are lean, we cook them on the bone and serve them pink.

Perhaps the foods we associate most with autumn are apples and pears. We like **Cox's apples** for *tarte Tatin* – Cox's make good tart fillings because they contain less water than other apple varieties. Their flavour is also brilliant in parfaits because it is so distinctive. We dry wafer-thin Cox's slices as chips or *tuiles*, to use as a decoration. Sometimes in the autumn we mix lightly poached apples with chopped prunes and serve topped with an apple gratinée .

The flavour of **pears** is beautifully rounded and needs little else in the way of flavouring. Comice, Williams' and Conference pears are all ideal for cooking, as long as they are slightly underripe and firm – too soft and they taste floury and have lost their edge of flavour. There are savoury uses for pears, such as in a fruit relish for foie gras (flavoured with a hint of saffron). For desserts, pears are great for poaching in a spiced red wine syrup to be served with a rich peppercorn-flavoured crème anglaise and, like apples, they make a good compote. Their flowery fragrance is also nicely complemented by a hint of lime. We also dry thin slices of pear, then sandwich them together with a cinnamon icecream, standing them upright on a compote of pears in red wine.

Lentil and langoustine soup

I do enjoy classic rustic dishes, especially those served with an elegant twist. This recipe is a lentil velouté served very thick and smooth and topped with roasted langoustines that float proud of the rich liquid underneath. I use the recipe as a 'teaser' to whet diners' appetites in my restaurant, but double or even treble the quantity will make a normal-size starter portion.

SERVES 4–6 AS A STARTER

250g Puy lentils

1 medium carrot, chopped in two or three

1 onion, quartered

1 fat clove garlic, peeled and left whole

1 fresh bouquet garni (bay leaf, sprig
   fresh thyme, some parsley stalks
   and celery leaves tied together)

1 litre Dark Chicken Stock (page 212)
   or Vegetable Nage (page 212)

a couple of drops of truffle oil

150ml double cream

8–12 raw langoustines, peeled

a few good pinches of curry powder

2 tablespoons olive oil

sea salt and freshly ground black pepper

1 Place the lentils (no need to soak) in a large saucepan with the vegetables, garlic and bouquet garni. Cover well with cold water and bring to the boil. Cook on a medium heat until the lentils just start to 'explode'. This should take about 15 minutes – no longer or they will turn mushy.

2 Drain the lentils, reserving about 250ml of the cooking liquid. Discard all the vegetables, garlic and bouquet garni. Purée the softened lentils in a food processor or blender, adding the reserved liquid to make a silky smooth purée.

3 Return to the pan and 'let down' with the stock or nage. Season and bring to the boil, stirring. Add the truffle oil and cream. That's it!

4 To cook the langoustines, dust them with the curry powder and seasoning. Heat a non-stick pan and, when you can feel a good heat rising, add the oil. Stir-fry the langoustines for a minute or so on each side until they turn pink and just firm.

5 Reheat the soup and pour into six warmed soup bowls. Top each serving with two langoustines and serve.

Potage of potato and leek

This is just the sort of soup someone learning to cook should begin with. But although simple it can be turned into the ultimate in sophistication simply by adding a few lightly poached oysters or topping with small spoonfuls of whipped cream and Osietra caviar. **SERVES 4 AS A STARTER**

250g leeks (the white and pale
  green only), diced
1 small onion, chopped
1 tablespoon olive oil
15g butter
50ml dry white wine
1 large potato, about 300g,
  peeled and chopped

1 fresh bouquet garni (a few parsley stalks,
  sprig fresh thyme, small bay leaf and
  sprig of celery leaves tied together)
750ml Light Chicken Stock (page 212)
  or Vegetable Nage (page 212)
100ml single cream
sea salt and freshly ground black pepper

1 Put the leeks and onion into a large saucepan with the oil and butter. When they start to sizzle, cover and sweat the vegetables over a low heat for 5 minutes.

2 Add the wine and cook uncovered until evaporated. Add the potato and bouquet garni, cover with the stock or nage and bring to the boil. Season and simmer for 15 minutes until the potato is soft.

3 Remove the bouquet garni. You can leave this soup chunky, as the vegetables are chopped small, and the potato should by now have dissolved into the liquid, thickening it slightly. However, if you favour a silky texture, then purée either in a food processor or blender, or in the pan with a hand-held stick blender.

4 Stir in the cream and season to taste. A good soup for any meal occasion.

Cauliflower and sorrel soup

A simple cream soup, this is ideal for when the nights start to draw in and you realise it's time to think about food for chilly weather. There are still leaves of spiky sorrel in the garden, and you don't need too many for this soup – just enough to lift the creamy colour. For a touch of class, treat your guests to a caviar garnish. In the summer you can serve this soup lightly chilled.

SERVES 6 AS A STARTER

1 large cauliflower, stalks discarded,
  florets chopped
1 medium potato, peeled and chopped
½ onion, chopped
15g butter
1 tablespoon olive oil
1 litre Light Chicken Stock (page 212)
  or Vegetable Nage (page 212)

500ml creamy milk
100ml double cream
6 large sorrel leaves, stalks trimmed
  and then shredded
2 tablespoons caviar (optional)
sea salt and freshly ground black pepper

1 Place the cauliflower florets, potato and onion in a saucepan with the butter and oil. Heat gently and, when the contents start to sizzle, cover with a lid and sweat everything over a low heat for about 10 minutes. The vegetables should not be at all coloured.

2 Add the stock or nage and bring to the boil, then pour in the milk and return gently to a boil. (This way, there will be no scum forming from the milk.) Season to taste, then simmer, uncovered, for 10–15 minutes when the vegetables should be soft.

3 Pour in half the cream, then purée in a food processor or blender, or whiz in the pan with a hand-held stick blender. Pass the purée through a sieve into a clean pan, rubbing with the back of a ladle.

4 Stir in the rest of the cream. Taste for seasoning and bring the soup to the boil. Ladle into soup plates, top with the sorrel shreds and add a spoonful of caviar to each. Serve straightaway.

A creamed soup of roasted ceps and garlic

At the end of the summer and into the early autumn, one can buy wonderful heads of garlic bursting with plump cloves – just the ingredient to complement the first of the autumn ceps. Garlic as a flavour is second to none, but it does have its minus points should you happen to love eating it in quantity – you soon find out who truly loves you. One way to enjoy your garlic and keep your friends is to blanch whole cloves several times in boiling water. The first boiling loosens the skins and so makes for easier peeling. When I can get hold of any, I garnish this soup with shredded leaves of Italian wild garlic. SERVES 4 AS A STARTER

1 head garlic, separated into cloves

3 tablespoons olive oil

1 shallot, finely chopped

150g fresh ceps, chopped

50ml dry white wine

1 small potato, peeled and diced small

1 fresh bouquet garni (a few parsley stalks, bay leaf, sprig fresh thyme and a few celery leaves tied together)

1 litre Dark Chicken Stock (page 212)

50ml double cream

sea salt and freshly ground black pepper

1 First, plunge the garlic cloves into a pan of boiling water. Boil for $^1/_2$ minute, then drain and refresh under cold running water. Slip the cloves out of their skins.

2 Replace the water in the pan with fresh. Bring to the boil and add the garlic. Boil briefly, then drain and refresh. Repeat a third time, then cool. Crush or chop finely. The garlic is now ready to use in the soup.

3 Heat the oil in a large saucepan and, when hot, add the shallot, ceps and garlic. Cook for about 10 minutes, stirring occasionally, until nicely caramelised. Deglaze with the wine and cook until evaporated, then stir in the chopped potato and bouquet garni. Cook for 2 minutes.

4 Pour in the stock and bring to the boil. Add seasoning to taste. Simmer for 15–20 minutes.

5 Remove the bouquet garni. Purée in a food processor or blender until smooth, then pass through a sieve into a clean pan, rubbing with the back of a ladle.

6 Reheat the soup and stir in the cream. Taste for seasoning and serve.

Wild duck salad
with hazelnut dressing

At the start of the game season you can buy small wild ducks with green necks (colverts), which are the size of a poussin. The flesh is much darker and more gamey than farmed duck. Although the legs are tough (it's all that summer swimming), the breasts make fine eating, especially in a warm salad with apple and celeriac. There are a number of stages to this recipe, but they are all simple and come together quickly at the end. SERVES 4 AS A STARTER OR LIGHT DISH

1 tablespoon olive oil

2 wild ducks, about 700g each

50g hazelnuts in skins

25g sultanas

200g celeriac

1 large, new season's Cox's apple

sea salt and freshly ground black pepper

Dressing

3 tablespoons groundnut oil

3 tablespoons hazelnut oil

1 tablespoon white wine vinegar

2 teaspoons sherry vinegar

a squeeze of lemon juice

1 Preheat the oven to 200°C, Gas 6. At the same time, heat the oil in a non-stick frying pan and brown the breasts of the birds, pressing the skin well onto the hot pan. Transfer the birds to a small roasting tin.

2 Roast the birds for 10–12 minutes, when the breasts should feel still slightly springy. You only need the breast meat so do not fret about the legs. Remove and set aside to rest for 15 minutes.

3 Meanwhile, roast the hazelnuts in the oven for about 10 minutes, watching them like a hawk so they do not burn, then rub them in a tea towel so the skins slip off. Chop the nuts. Soak the sultanas in boiling water to cover for 5 minutes so they plump up, then drain well.

4 Make the dressing by putting all the ingredients in a small jam jar, covering and shaking well to blend.

5 Peel the celeriac and cut into thin julienne strips. Mix with half the dressing, the sultanas and hazelnuts. Quarter, core and evenly chop the apple, leaving on the lovely blushed red and green skin. Mix with the celeriac salad.

6 Now, using a small, sharp filleting knife, slice off each duck breast in one piece. Carve each breast as thinly as you can. The flesh should be pink and lightly cooked. Lay the slices in a dish and season. Mix any of the duck juices that seep out with the rest of the dressing and drizzle over the duck breasts.

7 Lay the breast slices on top of the apple and celeriac salad, and serve as soon as possible.

Marinated tuna salad

Tuna is a dense, meaty fish so you need a smaller portion size than other fish, no more than 100g. The flesh is also affected by the way it is caught – the tail end is less likely to have any signs of congealed blood. So try to buy a piece of loin from the tail end. After searing in hot oil, marinate the tuna in a coriander-flavoured dressing. Then serve with soused autumnal vegetables. **SERVES 6 AS A STARTER OR 4 AS A LIGHT DISH**

400g loin of tuna, from the tail end

3 tablespoons olive oil

150ml Classic Vinaigrette (page 213)

1 teaspoon coriander berries, lightly crushed

1 tablespoon chopped fresh coriander

2 sticks salsify

a good squeeze of lemon juice

2 globe artichokes

100g mangetouts, chopped

1 small onion, sliced

2 medium carrots, thinly sliced

2 tablespoons aged balsamic vinegar

sea salt and freshly ground black pepper

1 Slice the tuna loin into two long fillets. Heat 1 tablespoon of the oil in a heavy-based frying pan (or a ridged griddle pan if you want attractive chargrilled stripes on the tuna). Sear the fillets for 2 minutes all over – the flesh should still feel a little springy. Do not overcook tuna, as it will toughen and dry out. Transfer to a dish.

2 Mix half the vinaigrette with the coriander berries, then pour over the tuna fillets. Press the fresh coriander over the surface. Cover and leave to steep for 1 hour.

3 Meanwhile, peel the salsify and cut into sticks. Cook in boiling salted water with the lemon juice for 5 minutes. Remove with a slotted spoon, refresh and set aside.

4 Cut off the artichoke stalks, pull off the leaves and cut out the hairy choke to leave the meaty heart. (See photographs of this technique on page 216.) Cut the heart into pieces. Cook in the lemon water for 10 minutes. Drain.

5 Blanch the mangetouts in boiling water for 1 minute, then drain and refresh under cold running water. Drain and pat dry.

6 Heat the remaining oil in a saucepan, add the onion and cook for 3 minutes. Add the carrots, salsify and artichokes, and cook for a further 2–3 minutes. Finally, toss in the blanched mangetouts and cook for 1 minute. Season nicely and stir in the basalmic vinegar and then the rest of the vinaigrette. Set aside to cool.

7 To serve, remove the tuna from the marinade (no need to scrape off the herbs unless you wish to). Cut the fillets into medallions. Divide the soused vegetables among the plates and place the tuna medallions on top of each.

Warm salad of pigeon
with honey-soused vegetables

Here is another starter that makes good use of the best foods in season. Root vegetables make delicious salads if marinated, then cooked briefly and left to cool in their juices. Game breasts cooked pink and sliced thinly complement it all nicely. **SERVES 4 AS A STARTER**

100g celeriac

100g kohlrabi

1 small bulb fennel

100g baby onions

2–3 tablespoons olive oil

100g baby carrots, scraped

50g tiny mushrooms, such as girolles
   or mousserons, trimmed

15g butter

8 boneless wood pigeon breasts,
   about 75g each

sea salt and freshly ground black pepper

Marinade

1 shallot, finely chopped

1 tablespoon olive oil

1 sprig fresh thyme (lemon thyme if possible)

1 tablespoon sherry vinegar

1 tablespoon flower honey

100ml groundnut oil

50ml hazelnut oil

juice of 1 lime

1 First, make the marinade. Gently sauté the shallot in the olive oil with the thyme for about 5 minutes until softened but not coloured. Deglaze with the vinegar and cook for a few seconds. Add the honey, groundnut and hazelnut oils, and the lime juice plus some seasoning. Keep warm.

2 Peel the celeriac and kohlrabi and cut into cubes or bâtons, varying the lengths and shapes to add interest. Keep the thicknesses even so the vegetables cook nicely. Peel the outside ribs of the fennel with a swivel peeler, then cut lengthways into wedges. Blanch the onions in boiling water for 2 minutes, then drain and peel.

3 Heat 1–2 tablespoons of olive oil in a heavy-based frying pan and stir in all the vegetables. Cook gently for 5–7 minutes, stirring occasionally, until they just begin to soften but without colouring them. Remove from the heat and pour over three-quarters of the marinade. Leave the vegetables to cool in this for at least 2 hours. Do not chill, as they should be at room temperature.

4 Now for the pigeon. Heat another tablespoon of olive oil with the butter in a heavy-based frying pan. Season the breasts and cook, skin side down, for about 3 minutes. Flip the breasts over and cook the other side for 2–3 minutes. They should feel lightly springy when pressed. Season again. Leave for 3 minutes or so whilst you dish the vegetables.

5 Drain the vegetables of their marinade (this can be re-used should you wish). Divide among four plates. Slice the pigeon breasts on the diagonal, or leave them whole, and sit on top of the vegetables. Trickle over some of the remaining marinade and serve hot.

Salad of ceps and langoustines in mustard dressing

Langoustines (aka Dublin Bay prawns) are sold in three sizes, from 1 to 3. I generally opt for the biggest, size 1, because the flesh is plump and sweet and remains moist when pan-roasted. To make them easier to peel, blanch just for 1 minute in boiling water. Apart from this, the salad is quite straightforward to prepare, and the colours and flavours come together so well on the plate. **SERVES 4 AS A STARTER**

12 large langoustines
3 tablespoons olive oil
200g large fresh ceps, bases trimmed,
   then thickly sliced
150ml Classic Vinaigrette (page 213)
1 slightly rounded tablespoon Dijon mustard
150g baby spinach leaves
a few good pinches of mild curry powder
sea salt and freshly ground black pepper
celery leaves, deep fried if you like, to garnish

1 Bring a large pan of salted water to the boil, then drop in the langoustines. Boil for a minute, then drain and cool. When you are able to handle them (they are easier to peel when warm), pull off the heads and crack the top of the shell with the back of a knife. Then simply push up from the tail end and out should pop perfectly peeled, pink shellfish. Set aside.

2 Heat 2 tablespoons of the oil in a frying pan and, when really hot, sauté the ceps until they are nicely coloured and softened. Season well. Remove and cool.

3 Mix the vinaigrette with the mustard. Toss the ceps with a third of the dressing. Set aside. Season the spinach and toss with another third of the dressing. Place in the centre of four plates. (In the restaurant we arrange the spinach leaves in a flower shape inside a large plain cutter – not possible, I know, when you are on your own.)

4 Season the langoustines and dust with pinches of curry power. Heat the last of the oil in a frying pan and, when really hot, sauté the langoustines quickly for a minute or two on each side. Cut each one in half, if large.

5 Spoon the mustardy ceps in the centre of the spinach, then top with the langoustines. Finally, trickle over the last of the dressing, garnish with celery leaves and serve quickly.

Salade tiède of mousserons, mussels and crosnes

This is a good example of a style of dish the French call 'terre et mer' – mixing foods of land and sea. It is a warm salad of mussels and two unusual ingredients found only during the autumn, mousserons and crosnes. Mousserons are tiny, perfectly formed mushrooms with caps the size of Smarties. Their fairy size gives a false impression, for they are tough little things and respond well to high frying. Crosnes, or Chinese artichokes, are 'wild' artichokes with a good earthy flavour. They both need particular preparation. **SERVES 4 AS A STARTER**

100g mousseron mushrooms
25g butter
2 tablespoons olive oil
300g fresh mussels
1 bay leaf
1 sprig fresh thyme
100ml dry white wine
100g crosnes (or use baby Jerusalem artichokes)
1 tablespoon chopped fresh chervil or parsley
2 tablespoons double cream
sea salt and freshly ground black pepper

1 Prepare this dish in stages, then bring everything together just before serving. First, the mousserons. Pick off the stalks so you just have the caps. Heat half the butter in a frying pan and sauté them for 2–3 minutes until softened.

2 Drain off the juice and save it in a small saucepan. Wipe out the frying pan, then heat the remaining butter with a teaspoon of the oil until nice and hot. Sauté the mousserons again to get them nice and browned. Drain, saving the juices again, and set aside.

3 Wash the mussels well and pull off any beards. Scrub off the barnacles too, if possible. Discard any mussels that don't close when you tap them. Heat an empty saucepan until very hot and tip in the mussels, together with the bay leaf, thyme and wine. Clamp on the lid and cook for about 4 minutes.

4 Uncover the pan and drain the liquid into the saucepan with the mousseron juices. Discard any mussels that haven't opened. Pick out the meat of those that have and cool, then chill for 30 minutes to firm the flesh.

5 To prepare the crosnes, top and tail if necessary, then place in a bowl with a little cold water and rub them between your hands with sea salt. This helps to scrub them clean. Rinse well.

6 Heat the remaining oil in a pan and sauté the crosnes until nicely coloured, about 3 minutes. Tip the mussels into the pan and stir-fry until reheated. Toss in the mousserons and reheat, then divide among four soup plates. Sprinkle with the chervil or parsley.

7 Add the cream to the saved juices and bubble down until reduced by half. Nappé the salad – there will be just enough sauce to moisten everything – and serve.

Pumpkin and pancetta risotto

It is a poor autumn kitchen indeed that does not have a plump pumpkin available. There are so many ways to take advantage of its creamy, sweet golden flesh, from soups and stews through to pasta fillings and dessert pies. A risotto with a lightly browned diced pumpkin brunoise, *some smoky crisp pancetta and tangy Parmesan makes a good light meal.* **SERVES 4 AS A STARTER OR 2 AS A MAIN DISH**

40g pancetta, chopped
500–600ml Light Chicken Stock (page 212)
2 large shallots, chopped
500g pumpkin flesh, cut into 1cm cubes
3 tablespoons olive oil
200g risotto rice (Carnaroli, Arborio or Vialone Nano)
100ml dry white wine
2 tablespoons mascarpone
25g freshly grated Parmesan cheese
sea salt and freshly ground black pepper

1 Heat a dry non-stick frying pan and, when hot, fry the pancetta until browned and crisp. Drain and set aside. Heat the stock to a gentle simmer in a saucepan.
2 In a large saucepan, gently sauté the shallots and pumpkin in the oil for about 5 minutes. Stir in the rice and cook for another 2 minutes to toast the grains. Pour in the wine and cook until reduced right down.
3 Now pour in a quarter of the stock and stir well. Cook gently until the liquid has been absorbed, then stir in another ladleful of stock. Continue cooking and stirring, gradually adding the stock, until the rice grains are just tender. The whole process should take about 15 minutes.
4 About 2 minutes before the end of cooking, stir in the pancetta, mascarpone and half of the Parmesan. Check the seasoning, then serve in warmed bowls, sprinkled with the remaining Parmesan.

Mosaic of autumn game

An attractive chunky terrine is the ultimate prepare-ahead starter. We don't use gelatine to set the layers, but rely instead on the natural setting properties of pork knuckles or trotters. You will need a nice selection of game birds and, maybe for a special treat, some foie gras.

When serving, we spread a touch of truffle oil on the top of each slice to give a nice inviting gloss. This terrine is best with toasted brioche, but crusty baguette would be fine. It is good too with an apple and celeriac salad such as that on page 121, or some mixed salad leaves dressed with a hazelnut vinaigrette. **MAKES A 1KG TERRINE TO SERVE 6–8 AS A STARTER**

2 gammon knuckles, or 700g collar
  bacon joint with 1 pig's trotter
1 carrot, roughly chopped
1 onion, roughly chopped
1 stick celery, roughly chopped
1 leek, roughly chopped
1 fresh bouquet garni (a bay leaf,
  sprig fresh thyme, parsley stalks
  and celery leaves tied together)
1 sprig fresh thyme

Meats
4 wood pigeon breasts
2 pheasant breasts
2 partridge breasts
2 free-range chicken breasts
200g venison fillet
3 tablespoons each Madeira,
  ruby Port and Cognac
2–3 tablespoons olive oil
sea salt and freshly ground black pepper

1 Put the gammon knuckles or bacon to soak overnight in plenty of cold water. For the meats, trim the breasts to neat shapes, discarding any skin, bone, fat or sinews. Toss them all together with the venison fillet and alcohol, and leave overnight to impart flavour and stain the flesh.
2 The next day, drain the knuckles or bacon and place in a large pan with the roughly chopped vegetables and bouquet garni (and the pig's trotter if using a bacon joint). Bring slowly to the boil, skimming off any scum that forms on top. Simmer for 1½–2 hours until the meat is very tender, skimming often. (It is the skimming that helps to give you a lovely clear stock.)
3 Leave the gammon or bacon to cool in the stock, then remove. Discard all skin and fat and pull the meat into thick shreds; set aside. Strain the stock, then bring to the boil and simmer with the fresh thyme sprig for about 10 minutes. Cool. Put some stock in a bowl and chill to test its setting strength. It should be firm. If not, boil the stock down to reduce further, and check for setting again. When it will set firm, measure out 500ml.
4 Drain the meats and pat dry. Heat the oil in a heavy-based frying pan and cook each meat separately: the chicken breasts for 4–5 minutes each side and the other meats for 3–4 minutes per side, depending on thickness. Cool on kitchen paper towel, adding seasoning as they cool.
5 Now assemble the terrine. Pour a little of the stock over the bottom of a 1kg terrine and allow to set in the fridge. Make your layers starting with thin slices of foie gras, if using, or a thin one of shredded gammon. Place the breasts, venison fillet and more shredded gammon lengthways on this. Spoon some of the setting stock over each layer – just enough the hold the meats in place. When you've finished, place the terrine in the fridge to set until firm, at least overnight.
6 To serve, dip the terrine mould briefly in a bowl of scalding hot water to the count of 5. Loosen the edges and shake out onto a board. Cut in thick slices with a warm long knife.

Tomato and Parmesan gratinée tarts

Autumn sees the abundance of plump, full-flavoured plum tomatoes, which I enjoy serving pizza-style on discs of light crisp pastry. The tomato slices are bound with melted Parmesan shavings and then placed on top of the pastry just before serving. A bouquet of rocket salad tops each tart. **SERVES 4 AS A STARTER**

300g puff pastry, preferably home-made (page 214)
8 large, ripe plum tomatoes, skinned
2 tablespoons balsamic vinegar
2 tablespoons olive oil
1 tablespoon chopped fresh chervil
1 tablespoon chopped fresh parsley
50g fresh Parmesan, shaved with a swivel peeler
100g wild rocket
1–2 tablespoons Classic Vinaigrette (page 213)
sea salt and freshly ground black pepper

1 Roll out the pastry to a thickness of a £1 coin. Cut out four rounds about 12cm diameter, using a saucer or small plate as a guide. Place on a heavy baking sheet and chill for 20 minutes.
2 Preheat the oven to 200°C, Gas 6. Bake the pastry for 10 minutes, then place another baking sheet on top to press the rounds down and keep them flat. Bake for a further 8–10 minutes until just golden. Remove to a wire rack to cool and crisp.
3 Slice the tomatoes evenly and arrange on another baking sheet in four overlapping circles about the same size as the pastry rounds (certainly no larger). Brush with the balsamic vinegar and oil, season and sprinkle with the herbs. Lay the shavings of Parmesan on top, making sure they connect with all the tomato slices – as they melt, the shavings will hold the tomato together.
4 Preheat the grill to the highest setting. When really hot, place the tomatoes under the grill near to the heat. The cheese should start to melt almost immediately. Watch carefully – the cheese doesn't need to brown, just melt so it holds the tomato slices together.
5 Remove from the grill and wait a few seconds, then using a fish slice transfer each round of tomato onto a pastry round.
6 Season the rocket and toss with the vinaigrette. Pile on top of each tart and serve immediately.

Saffron red mullet on vegetables à la grecque

Red mullet, as you may have gathered, is one of my favourite foods. It not only tastes good, the thin red skin looks so inviting, and it gives me great scope to cook it in so many ways. You will need small fishes if possible for this recipe, or failing that two larger ones about 500g each, with fillets cut in half. The fish is served on vegetables in a spicy oil marinade – a great casual main meal. The same idea works well with very fresh mackerel. Grelots are squat onions popular in France. Tubby shallots will do if you can't find them. **SERVES 4 AS A MAIN DISH**

4 small red mullets, about 250g each,
  neatly filleted in two, skin on
5 tablespoons olive oil
2 generous pinches of saffron strands
4 baby fennels, or 2 medium ones
2 medium carrots, thinly sliced
8 grelot onions or 4 fat shallots, sliced
sea salt and freshly ground black pepper

Marinade
150ml olive oil
1 tablespoon white wine vinegar
1 tablespoon aged balsamic vinegar
6 coriander seeds, roughly crushed
6 white peppercorns, roughly crushed
1–4 star anise
4 whole cloves
6 sprigs fresh coriander

1 Heat all the ingredients for the marinade until on the point of boiling, then set aside to infuse for 10–15 minutes.

2 Meanwhile, prepare the mullets. Trim the fillets neatly, feeling for any pin bones with the tips of your fingers and pulling them out with tweezers or your fingernails. (If the fillets are large, then cut each across in two.) Rub both sides with 2 tablespoons of the olive oil and season. Crush the saffron strands on top of the pretty pink skin side. Set aside to marinate for 5–10 minutes.

3 If using baby fennel, trim and cut each in half lengthways. If using larger bulbs, cut into quarters. Sauté the fennel in the remaining 3 tablespoons of olive oil for 3–5 minutes, then add the carrots and sauté for 2 minutes. Finally, add the onions (or shallots) and sauté for a further 2 minutes. Remove the vegetables to a shallow serving dish, season and pour over the marinade. Leave to cool to room temperature.

4 Heat a large non-stick frying pan and, when you can feel a good heat rising, place the

fillets in, saffron-crusted skin side down. Cook on this side for 5 minutes until the flesh
feels nearly firm and the skin is nice and crispy. Carefully flip the fillets over, taking care
not to tear the skin, and cook the other side for a minute or two. Season well.

5 Slip each cooked fillet gently into the dish and spoon over the vegetables and marinade
to cover. Cool the fish to room temperature. Carefully pour off the marinade. (The marinade
can be strained and stored in the fridge for up to a week to be used again.)

6 Serve the mullet fillets and marinated vegetables at room temperature or lightly chilled.
This dish is good with a lightly dressed rocket salad.

Red mullet with orange-glazed fennel and pesto dressing

Fennel is a popular vegetable all over the Mediterranean – market stalls and farmers' carts are often piled high with crisp, fresh bulbs, full of juicy aniseed flavour. Our use of it is often restricted to salads or, occasionally, cooking with a tomato sauce. But there are many other flavours of the sun it complements. Orange is one, pesto another and, of course, it is one of the great fish accompaniments. This meal combines all these elements. SERVES 4 AS A MAIN DISH

4 medium red mullets, 250–300g each,
    neatly filleted in two, skin on
2 good pinches of saffron strands,
    finely crushed
3 tablespoons Classic Vinaigrette (page 213)
2 large bulbs fennel
4 tablespoons olive oil
1 teaspoon fine sea salt
1 teaspoon caster sugar
200ml fresh orange juice

15g butter
sea salt and freshly ground black pepper

Pesto
25g pine kernels
2 fat cloves garlic, roughly chopped
15g leaves fresh basil
50g Parmesan cheese, freshly grated
3 tablespoons extra virgin olive oil

1 Neaten the edges of the mullet fillets. Check the flesh for pin bones and pull them out. Rub the crushed saffron over the pink skin. Set aside in the fridge.

2 Make the pesto in a food processor, whizzing all the ingredients together. Mix with the vinaigrette. Set aside.

3 To prepare the fennel, trim the tops, then using a small sharp knife, shave off the rough ribs. Cut each bulb in half lengthways. Cut out the core, but leave the root end intact, to hold the layers together. (See photographs of this technique on page 219.)

4 Preheat the oven to 190°C, Gas 5. Heat 2 tablespoons of the oil in a large flameproof pan that can be used in the oven. Mix the salt and sugar together and sprinkle over the fennel. Add the fennel halves to the pan, pressing them firmly into the hot oil, and turn once or twice to colour them well all over. Deglaze with the orange juice and slip the knob of butter down the side of the pan. Spoon the juices over the fennel.

5 Cover with a butter paper and transfer to the oven. Cook for 15–20 minutes until the fennel is softened, basting at least twice with the pan juices. Check the tenderness with the tip of a sharp knife.

6 While the fennel is cooking, heat the remaining 2 tablespoons of oil in a large heavy-based pan and fry the mullet fillets for a good 3 minutes on the skin side. Carefully flip the fillets over and cook the other side briefly, about 1 minute. Mullet is a delicate fish, so treat it carefully. Remove and keep warm.

7 Lift the fennel halves onto a board. Make neat cuts from root to tip, keeping the root uncut so it keeps the fennel halves together. Transfer to warmed plates and press the 'fans' open. Lay two mullet fillets on top of each fennel fan and drizzle around the pesto dressing.

Brill fillets with a confit of ceps and tomato

Brill is becoming increasingly easier to find in good fishmongers. A flat fish with a firm texture, it must always be skinned before cooking – and with very hard, tiny scales, it has one of the worst skins to prepare. The fish is served with two confits – tomatoes done in olive oil and ceps in goose fat. Both are brilliant with brill. **SERVES 4 AS A MAIN DISH**

6 large plum tomatoes, skinned
3–4 tablespoons olive oil
2 cloves garlic, sliced
leaves from 1 sprig fresh thyme
4 fillets of brill, about 125g each, skinned
200g baby spinach leaves
15g butter
¼ quantity Confit of Ceps (page 213)
  with some of the fat
1–2 tablespoons olive oil
a good squeeze of lemon juice
sea salt and freshly ground black pepper

1 First, make the tomato confit. Preheat the oven to 150°C, Gas 2. Quarter the tomatoes, cut out the cores and scoop out the seeds. Neaten into 'petal' shapes (you should have 24 all told) and place in a small roasting tin. Drizzle over the oil, and scatter on the garlic slices, thyme leaves and seasoning. Slow roast the tomatoes for about 1 hour, basting two or three times, until they are softened but still hold their shape. Allow to cool to room temperature.
2 Neaten the brill fillets if necessary and check the flesh for pin bones by running your fingers against the flesh.
3 Blanch the spinach in a little boiling salted water with the butter. When it has just wilted, remove and drain well, pressing down with the back of a ladle. Keep warm.
4 Put the confit of ceps, with some of the fat, in a small pan and reheat gently.
5 Meanwhile, heat the oil in a large non-stick frying pan. Season the fish and cook for about 3 minutes on each side until it feels just firm. Squeeze over the lemon juice.
6 To serve, place the spinach in a mound in the centre of four warmed plates. Sit the brill fillets on top. Arrange the ceps confit around the outside and sit six tomato petals on top of the confit. Drizzle around a teaspoon of the ceps fat for each serving.

Roasted cod with garlic pomme purée

Chunky cod with creamed potatoes is one of our national culinary treasures, especially if cooked perfectly. Cod fillets from a fish about 4–5kg in weight give perfect texture – any larger and the flakes of flesh become too big and won't hold together after cooking. Did you know cod is the fish with the least amount of scales? This means the skin can be scored easily. We take advantage of this and insert 'cloutes' of herbs – thyme or rosemary sprigs or rolled-up basil leaves – through the skin. For the garlic potato, blanch and refresh the garlic cloves at least three times so you get the flavour without pungency. SERVES 4 AS A MAIN DISH

2 large potatoes (such as Desirée
  or Maris Piper)
6 large cloves garlic
150ml milk
4 tablespoons double cream
75g butter
100g large fresh ceps, trimmed
  and thinly sliced

juice of ½ lemon
1 tablespoon olive oil
4 large *tranches* of cod (thick, neat
  pieces of fillet), 175–200g each, skin on
sea salt and freshly ground black pepper

1 Peel the potatoes and cut into even-size dice. Cook in boiling salted water for 12–15 minutes. Drain well, then return to the pan and dry out for 1–2 minutes over the heat. Mash the flesh or press through a potato ricer back into the pan.

2 While the potatoes are cooking, blanch the garlic in boiling water for a minute, then drain and refresh in cold water. Repeat the blanching twice more, then peel off the skin and mash the cloves to a purée on a small plate using a saucer. Mix into the potato.

3 Scald the milk and slowly stir into the potato purée with some seasoning. Then slowly add the cream to make a nice, velvety smooth purée. Cook out gently for 5 minutes, then gradually beat in half the butter which has been cut into small dice.

4 Meanwhile, heat the remaining butter in a saucepan and gently fry the ceps for about 4 minutes. Add the lemon juice and toss well until piping hot.

5 Heat the oil in a heavy-based frying pan and add the fish, skin side down. Cook for 6–7 minutes until just firm, then flip the *tranches* over and cook briefly on the other side – 90% of the cooking time should be on the skin side.

6 To serve, place the pomme purée in the middle of four dinner plates, set the cod on top and scatter the ceps around.

Monkfish with creamy curried mussels

This is a chunky, yet light and creamy main meal 'soup', perfect for a blustery day when you'd like a dish of warming comfort food. The monkfish fillets are dusted in curry spices before roasting, which gives them an appetising colour and crust. **SERVES 4 AS A MAIN DISH**

1 large tail of monkfish, 450–500g,
  filleted in two
250g mussels
1 bay leaf
1 sprig fresh thyme
50ml dry white wine
1 carrot, finely diced
1 small leek, finely diced
1 small stick celery, finely diced

2 tablespoons olive oil
2 teaspoons mild curry powder
2 pinches of saffron strands, crushed
300ml Noilly Prat
300ml Fish Stock (page 212)
300ml double cream
100g baby leaf spinach, shredded
sea salt and freshly ground black pepper

1 Trim off as much of the grey membrane from the monkfish as possible. (It is important to do this so the fish does not curl during cooking.) Cut each fillet in half lengthways so you have four fillets about 100g each. Set aside and chill.

2 Scrub the mussels and remove beards, if necessary. Discard any that don't close when tapped. Heat a large pan until very hot, then tip in the mussels with the thyme and wine. Clamp on the lid and cook for 3–4 minutes, shaking the pan once or twice. Uncover and discard any mussels that are still closed. Strain off the juices and reserve. Remove the mussel meat from the shells.

3 Sauté the diced carrot, leek and celery (*mirepoix*) in 1 tablespoon of the oil for about 5 minutes until softened. Add 1 teaspoon of the curry powder and the saffron and cook for a few seconds, then pour in the Noilly Prat. Cook until reduced right down to a syrupy consistency. Add the stock and reserved mussel juices and cook until reduced by half. Stir in the cream and simmer for 5 minutes. Season nicely and mix in the mussels and spinach. Reheat and keep the 'soup' hot.

4 Dust the monkfish fillets with salt and the remaining curry powder. Heat the remaining oil in a non-stick frying pan and, when nice and hot, sear the fish in the hot oil, turning to brown evenly. Cook for 3–4 minutes on each side until the flesh firms enough to feel just lightly springy when pressed with the back of a fork. Season again. Remove and allow to rest for 3–4 minutes, then slice into medallions if you like.

5 Divide the 'soup' among four warmed soup plates. Arrange the monkfish on top and serve hot.

John Dory with ratatouille vegetables and white beans

We tend to think of aubergines, peppers and courgettes as early autumn vegetables – grown naturally, they are in abundance at this time of year. I 'marry' them with some nicely cooked haricot beans, then serve with some pan-fried fillets of John Dory. This fish is best cooked with its skin on – the flesh parts into three segments, so the skin is necessary to hold the fillets together. The sauce is made with chicken stock. I often serve meat stocks with full-flavoured fish. Incidentally, you can cook double or even treble the amount of beans and freeze what you don't use. It makes sound kitchen sense to cook a larger batch. SERVES 4 AS A MAIN DISH

100g dried haricot beans,
  soaked overnight
½ small onion
1 small carrot, halved
2 sprigs fresh thyme
1 aubergine
2 medium courgettes
4 red peppers

4 yellow peppers
3 tablespoons olive oil
500ml Dark Chicken Stock (page 212)
150ml double cream
4 fillets of John Dory, about 120g each,
  skin on
sea salt and freshly ground black pepper

1 Drain the soaked beans and place in a pan of cold water. Bring to the boil and hold the boil for 10 minutes. Then drain and cover with fresh cold water. Add the onion, carrot and 1 sprig of thyme. Bring to the boil, then simmer for 45–55 minutes until the beans are just tender but still whole. Drain, and discard the onion, carrot and thyme. Season the beans as they cool.

2 Cut off the skin of the aubergine in 1.5cm thick lengths. You want nicely coloured strips of vegetable, with skin. Discard the inner flesh or use it elsewhere. Cut the aubergine strips into triangles about 2.5cm on all sides. Do the same with the courgettes.

3 Peel the skin from the whole peppers using a swivel vegetable peeler. Cut off the flesh in long pieces and discard the cores. Cut the pepper flesh into triangles too.

4 Heat 2 tablespoons of the oil in a frying pan and gently sauté the aubergines for about 3 minutes. Add the peppers and sauté for 2 minutes, then add the courgettes and sauté for a further 2–3 minutes. Season nicely. Ladle in about 100ml of the stock, and add a few of the remaining thyme leaves. Simmer uncovered until the liquid reduces right down and coats the vegetables in a glossy glaze. Stir in the haricots and reheat gently.

5 While the vegetables are cooking, boil the remaining stock until reduced by half. Add the cream and the last of the thyme leaves, and cook for 5 minutes. Season to taste.

6 Finally, heat the last of the oil in a large non-stick frying pan. Season the fish and cook it on the skin side for 3 minutes until nicely browned. Carefully turn the fillets over and cook the other side for 2 minutes or until just firm but still a little springy.

7 Divide the vegetables among four warmed plates, sit a fish fillet on top of each and pour the sauce around.

Confit of duck legs

There's something very appealing about slow-cooked duck that is meltingly tender and falling away from the bone. I use Gressingham duck, with its slightly lean and full-flavoured meat. You can buy the legs separately, and these are particularly good cooked confit-style in goose fat, then served with chips and a salad of frisée. **SERVES 4 AS A MAIN DISH**

leaves from 1 sprig fresh thyme
4 duck legs (preferably Gressingham duck)
about 500g goose fat
1 fresh bouquet garni (bay leaf, few
   parsley stalks, sprig fresh thyme and
   a small stick celery tied together)
200g frisée leaves
Classic Vinaigrette (page 213)
Chips (see My Special Steak Tartare
   and Chips, page 197), to serve
sea salt and freshly ground black pepper

1 Press the leaves of fresh thyme onto the duck legs and sprinkle with sea salt. Leave at room temperature for 1 hour to draw out some moisture. In the meantime, preheat the oven to 160°C, Gas 3.
2 Put the duck legs and goose fat in a pan and heat gently until just on the point of boiling. Transfer to a shallow casserole and add the bouquet garni. Cover and place in the oven. Slow roast for about 1½ hours until you can loosen the leg bone fairly easily. This indicates the meat is nicely tender.
3 Drain the legs and dab with kitchen paper towel. Strain the fat and keep for sautéeing potatoes and other uses – it is delicious. Heat a dry heavy-based frying pan and, when hot, cook the legs skin side down for a few minutes to crisp the skin. Take care not to overcook.
4 Dress the frisée with a little vinaigrette and place in the centre of four plates. Arrange the chips around the edge, then place the crispy duck legs on top of the leaves.

Saddle of rabbit with herb gnocchi

This is a good country dish served with style. Like duck, you can slow-cook rabbit in goose fat until the meat is deliciously tender. Once cooked, the meat can be served with home-made potato gnocchi and some oven-roasted tomatoes. A lovely, lazy lunch course.

SERVES 4 AS A MAIN DISH

1 saddle of rabbit, about 500g
1 tablespoon olive oil
leaves from 1 sprig fresh rosemary, chopped
400g goose fat
mixed salad leaves, to garnish
sea salt and freshly ground black pepper

Gnocchi
2 large baking potatoes (Desirée or
  Maris Piper), about 400g each
160g plain flour
1 teaspoon fine sea salt
1 large free-range egg
1 tablespoon each chopped fresh basil
  and parsley
3–4 tablespoons olive oil

1 Take the 2 long fillets from the saddle of rabbit. Wrap each tightly in cling film and chill for 24 hours.

2 The next day, unwrap the rabbit fillets and rub lightly with the oil, then sprinkle the surface with a little salt and chopped rosemary leaves. Leave for 1 hour.

3 Place the rabbit and goose fat in a shallow heavy-based saucepan. Bring to the boil, then reduce the heat to the lowest possible – whatever you can get it down to will be okay. Cook for 1–1¼ hours, possibly more, until the meat is tender. Allow the rabbit to cool in the fat, then lift out and dab dry with kitchen paper towel. Keep the fat for other recipes.

4 While the rabbit is cooking, make the gnocchi. Preheat the oven to 180°C, Gas 4. Bake the potatoes for about 1 hour until cooked. (Baking keeps the flesh dry.) Cool, then scoop out the flesh and mash or press through a potato ricer. Mix with the flour, salt, egg and herbs. Gradually work in 3 tablespoons of the oil until you have a firm, but still soft dough.

5 Turn out onto a cold floured surface and knead gently until smooth. Roll into a long cigar shape, wrap in cling film, and allow to rest and cool.

6 Bring a large pan of salted water to the boil and add the remaining oil. Using the back of a table knife (this helps to squash the ends to a traditional gnocchi shape), cut off 3cm lengths. (See photographs of this technique on page 220.) Drop straight into the simmering water and cook for about 3 minutes.

7 Have ready a large bowl of iced water. As each batch of gnocchi is cooked, lift out with a slotted spoon and dunk straight into the iced water. Leave for a minute or so, then drain well and pat dry with kitchen paper towel.

8 When ready to serve, preheat the grill. When it is hot, brown the rabbit fillets lightly on all sides. Meanwhile, heat some oil or goose fat in a frying pan and fry the cooked gnocchi for 3–4 minutes until crispy on both sides. Drain on kitchen paper towel.

9 Cut each rabbit fillet diagonally in half and serve with the gnocchi and a salad leaf garnish.

Veal rump with a fricassée of ceps and cabbage

This is a good party dish. You can par-cook the vegetables ahead, then reheat while you pan-fry the tender, lean veal rumps just before serving. Veal rumps, which come from the top of the leg, are best marinated for a good 6 hours before cooking. SERVES **4** AS A MAIN DISH

4 steaks of veal rump, about 120g each
4 tablespoons olive oil
1 large bay leaf, crushed
2 sprigs fresh thyme
200g large fresh ceps, bases trimmed
2 medium plum tomatoes, skinned and seeded
1 medium Savoy cabbage
50g butter
2 tablespoons chopped fresh chives
3 tablespoons Classic Vinaigrette (page 213)
sea salt and freshly ground black pepper

1 Trim the veal steaks to neaten, if necessary. Place in a shallow dish and drizzle over half the oil. Tuck the crushed bay leaf and the leaves from 1 thyme sprig between the steaks. Leave to marinate in the fridge for 6 hours.

2 Slice the ceps evenly but not too thinly. Finely chop the tomatoes. Quarter the cabbage, discarding the first layer of outer leaves. Cut out the cabbage core, then shred the leaves finely.

3 Bring a large pan of salted water to the boil and blanch the cabbage for 2 minutes. Drain and refresh under cold running water, then drain well again. Heat the butter in the same pan and add the thyme leaves from the second sprig. Cook for a few seconds, then toss in the blanched cabbage. Stir well and cook for a further 2 minutes until nicely glazed and cooked. Season well, then set aside.

4 Heat the remaining oil in a frying pan and sauté the sliced ceps for about 5 minutes until lightly browned and just tender. Toss in the diced tomato and chives, and season. Mix with the cabbage. Keep hot.

5 Heat a large non-stick frying pan. Lift the veal steaks out of the dish and drain off the oil. Season lightly. Cook the steaks for 2–3 minutes on each side until the meat feels lightly springy when pressed with the back of a fork. Do not overcook – veal should be served 'just above pink'. Remove and allow to rest for a few minutes. Swirl the vinaigrette into the pan to deglaze the juices.

6 To serve, divide the vegetables among four plates. Slice the steaks thinly on the diagonal and arrange on top of the vegetables. Nappé with the pan *jus* and serve.

Sweetbreads with shallot and mushroom marmalade

Few home cooks bother with sweetbreads these days, which is a great shame. Prepared like this, they are deliciously creamy inside with a crispy coating. Whenever I put the dish on the menu it is very popular, so I know there are people who love to eat them. Buy the pancreas sweetbreads, also known as 'heartbreads'. Some recipes tell you to blanch sweetbreads first and then peel off the membrane. I find it easier to use a razor-sharp thin knife instead. Allow one pair of sweetbreads for two people. **SERVES 4 AS A MAIN DISH**

2 pairs sweetbreads, 250–300g each
1 teaspoon mild curry powder
2 tablespoons olive oil
50ml Classic Vinaigrette (page 213)
200g wild rocket
sea salt and freshly ground black pepper

Marmalade
250g large shallots (banana shallots),
    thinly sliced
4 tablespoons olive oil
1 tablespoon demerara sugar
$^1/_2$ teaspoon fresh thyme leaves
2 tablespoons sherry vinegar
50ml Classic Vinaigrette (page 213)
150g chestnut mushrooms, thinly sliced

1 Make the marmalade first. Sauté the shallots in 2 tablespoons of the oil for 10 minutes, then stir in the sugar and carry on cooking until the shallots become caramelised, juicy and softened. Stir in the thyme, vinegar and vinaigrette, and season.

2 In a separate pan, heat the remaining oil and, when hot, sauté the mushrooms for about 5 minutes until softened. Season, then stir into the shallots. Set aside.

3 Skin the sweetbreads of their membranes using the tip of a very sharp knife and working it in a sawing motion. Cut each pair of sweetbreads in half, then dust lightly with salt and the curry powder.

4 Heat the oil in a frying pan and cook the sweetbreads for 7–8 minutes, turning once or twice. Make sure the outsides are nice and crispy. Trickle in half of the vinaigrette and carry on cooking for a couple of minutes, stirring to coat the sweetbreads lightly with the pan juices. Remove and drain on kitchen paper towel.

5 Toss the rocket in the last of the vinaigrette and season nicely. Divide the marmalade among four plates and place the dressed rocket on top. Sit the sweetbreads on the rocket and serve immediately.

Roasted autumn fruits

Choose a selection of the best seasonal fresh fruits and turn them into a new fruit salad with style! Tossing the fruits first in icing sugar and then pan-roasting them in a stinking hot pan gives them a delicious caramelised flavour. Absolutely fabulous with thick cream. **SERVES 4–6**

50g caster sugar

1 small glass Champagne or other
   dry white sparkling wine

2 large Conference pears

4 large red plums

2 Cox's apples

a good handful of blackberries
   or fresh cranberries

25g icing sugar

2 tablespoons *eau-de-vie*,
   or brandy or whisky

1 Dissolve the caster sugar in 100ml water, then boil for 3 minutes. Remove from the heat and add the Champagne or sparkling wine. Pour into a large bowl and set aside.

2 Peel and core the pears, then slice or chop. Halve the plums, stone and slice. Core and slice the apples.

3 Heat a large non-stick frying pan until really hot. Meanwhile, mix all the fruits together in a bowl and toss gently with the icing sugar.

4 Stir-fry the sugar-dusted fruits in the hot pan for about 1 minute, then add the *eau-de-vie* or other spirit and cook for a minute or two until evaporated.

5 Slide the hot fruits into the Champagne syrup. Leave until cool, then chill lightly. Serve with whipped cream and thin crispy biscuits, such as Coconut Tuiles (page 215).

Meringues with vanilla and autumn berry cream

Here's a recipe for those of you who have a sweet tooth and love creamy puddings. Make round discs of meringues with crisp outers and gooey insides and, to make them extra wicked, coat the bases with chocolate. Sandwich together with whipped cream and crushed berries – a mixture of the last of the late-summer strawberries and raspberries, some blackberries and a handful of hedgerow elderberries. SERVES **6**

4 large free-range egg whites
pinch of fine sea salt
250g caster sugar, plus 2 teaspoons for cream
100g dark chocolate (optional)
1 vanilla pod, slit in half
about 300ml double cream
200g mixed strawberries, raspberries,
   blackberries and elderberries, lightly crushed
1 small ripe mango, peeled and chopped

1 Make the meringues first. Put the egg whites and salt into a large, completely clean mixing bowl. Using an electric mixer, start whisking slowly, then gradually increase the speed. Whisk steadily until you have softly stiff, glossy white peaks. The mixture should be firm, but not dry and granular. Whisk in a tablespoon or two of the sugar, and when that is incorporated whisk in another spoonful. Carry on whisking in the sugar until all of the 250g is mixed in. Spoon the meringue mixture into a piping bag fitted with a plain nozzle about 1.5–2cm diameter.

2 Preheat the oven to its lowest setting, about 140°C, Gas 1. Line a baking tray (or two) with non-stick parchment or a silicone cooking liner. Pipe the meringue mixture into 12cm concentric ring discs, aiming for a 1cm thickness. You should have at least 12 discs.

3 Bake the meringues for 1½–2 hours until the outsides are firm and crisp but the insides still feel a little squidgy. Remove the baking tray to a wire rack. After 10 minutes, slide the meringues off the paper or liner onto the wire rack to cool completely.

4 Melt the chocolate, if using, either in a pan over hot water or in the microwave. Cool a little, then spread over the underside of the meringues. Set them upside down on the wire rack.

5 Slit the vanilla pod lengthways and scrape out the tiny, sticky seeds into the cream. Add the 2 teaspoons of sugar and whip until thick and smooth but not stiff. Fold enough cream into the fruits to bind them together.

6 Just before serving, sandwich together pairs of meringues with the fruit cream.

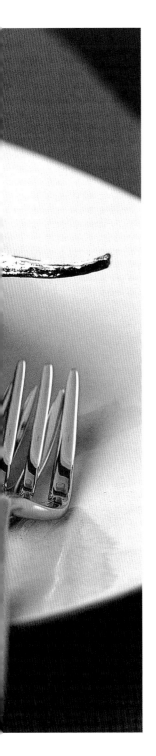

Caramelised apple tart

Making a fruit tart with crisp pastry and tender fruit can be tricky. The answer is to bake it upside down, so the fruit juices do not leach into the pastry and make it soggy. Ideally, make this tart in a shallow metal pan that will go into the oven, such as a gratin pan, paella pan or proper tarte Tatin tin (in the restaurant, we make individual tarts and decorate with a slit vanilla pod dusted with icing sugar). Serve with some scoops of a rich vanilla icecream, or try home-made Thyme Icecream (page 214), Fromage Blanc Sorbet (page 215), Lemon Sorbet (page 215) or quenelles of mascarpone or clotted cream. **SERVES 2–3**

3 large Cox's apples
300g Puff Pastry (page 214)
40g cold unsalted butter, thinly sliced
80g caster sugar mixed with
　¼ teaspoon Chinese five-spice powder

1 About 4 hours before cooking, quarter the apples, cut out the core and peel thinly. Leave the apple quarters uncovered so they oxidise a little and dry out. It doesn't matter if they brown because, of course, they will be coated in a caramel anyway.
2 Roll out the pastry and cut out a circle 23–24cm in diameter (this is assuming you will be making a tart of 20–21cm diameter). You may find it helpful to use a large round cake tin as a template. Prick lightly with the tip of a sharp knife and chill for an hour or two.
3 Preheat the oven to 200°C, Gas 6. When ready to cook, layer the thinly sliced hard butter in the bottom of your pan and sprinkle over the spiced sugar. Press the apple quarters into the butter, cored side uppermost, arranging them in a circle with one in the centre.
4 Place the pan over a medium heat. After a few minutes, start to roll the pan so the butter and sugar dissolve and mix together. Tip the pan occasionally so you can check that the caramel is forming. Cook like this for a total of 10 minutes, then remove from the heat.
5 Lay the pastry over the pan and tuck the edges down inside, pressing in with a fork. Place the pan in the oven (take care because the caramel will be hot and could dribble down your arm – you must avoid chef's arms!). Bake for about 15 minutes until the pastry is golden brown and crisp. Remove and cool before up-ending onto a large round platter. If the caramel sticks fast, then reheat it for a few minutes to melt.

Pear, honey and lime cake

I do enjoy homely cakes, and this is becoming a fast favourite with my family. It's a combination of a traditional Victoria sponge and a French tarte bourdaloue. Eat it as a teatime treat, or serve warm with cream for dessert. **SERVES 6**

50g unsalted butter
3 Comice pears, peeled, halved and cored
5 tablespoons light flower honey
grated zest and juice of 2 limes
1 vanilla pod
100ml pear *eau-de-vie*

Cake
175g unsalted butter, softened
  to room temperature
175g caster sugar
1 teaspoon baking powder
a good pinch of salt
4 large free-range eggs, beaten
175g plain flour, sifted

1 Melt the 50g of butter in a shallow pan and cook the pears for about 5 minutes until they take on a light golden colour, turning once or twice. Stir in the honey, lime juice and vanilla pod. Cook for a further 2 minutes or so, then stir in the *eau-de-vie*. Remove from the heat and leave the pears to steep in the syrup until cool, about 3 hours.

2 To make the cake mixture, beat the butter and sugar with the lime zest until smooth, then mix in the baking powder and salt. Gradually work in the beaten eggs, then, using a large metal spoon, fold in the sifted flour. Cover the bowl with cling film and set aside to rest for 45 minutes.

3 When ready to bake, preheat the oven to 200°C, Gas 6. Grease and line a 23cm round cake tin that is about 6cm deep.

4 Drain the pears and pat lightly dry. Reserve the syrup. Slash 3 of the halves evenly into slices, keeping them attached at the thin end in the shape of pear halves. Chop the remaining pears and stir into the cake mixture. Spoon the cake mixture into the tin, level the top and place the slashed pear halves on top.

5 Bake for 10 minutes. Reduce the oven temperature to 150°C, Gas 2, and continue baking for 45–50 minutes until the top of the cake feels lightly springy. Test if it is cooked by pushing a long thin wooden stick into the centre; it should come out clean. Leave the cake to cool for 15 minutes in the tin, then turn out onto a wire rack and cool completely.

6 If liked, skewer the cake a few times and spoon over 4–6 tablespoons of the pear syrup. Brush the top of the slashed pears with some syrup before serving.

Pear and frangipane flan

This classic dessert is always popular and, more to the point, easy to make. I always roll out far more pastry than is needed to line the tin, to allow for shrinkage. This way the filling can be completely level with the top of the pastry case, with no dips or gaps. Serve warm with crème fraîche or a trickle of double cream. **SERVES 6**

3 even-size firm pears (such as
   Williams' or Comice)
600ml Stock Syrup (page 214)
1 vanilla pod, slit open

Pastry
100g unsalted butter, softened
   to room temperature
70g caster sugar
1 vanilla pod
1 medium free-range egg, beaten
200g plain flour sifted with
   a large pinch of fine sea salt

Filling
100g ground almonds
100g caster sugar
100g unsalted butter
20g plain flour
2 large free-range eggs, beaten
2 tablespoons dark rum
a little icing sugar infused with
   a sprig fresh rosemary

1 First, poach the pears. Peel thinly, halve and core. Bring the stock syrup to the boil, add the vanilla and then slip in the pears. Turn the heat right down and poach gently for 10–12 minutes until softened. Remove, drain and cool. (The syrup can be strained, cooled and chilled for re-use.)

2 Now, make the pastry. Beat the butter with the sugar until smooth and creamy. Slit the vanilla pod and scrape out the seeds with the tip of a sharp knife. Add to the mixture. Work in the beaten egg and flour alternately until you have a smooth dough. Knead lightly, then wrap in cling film and chill for 20 minutes or so.

3 Roll out the dough as thinly as you are able, to a round about 30cm in diameter, large enough to line a 21cm flan tin, about 2.5–3cm deep, comfortably with overhang. You could do this on a lightly floured board, or between two lightly floured sheets of cling film. Lift the dough on the rolling pin into the flan tin (or a flan ring set on a heavy, flat baking sheet). Press the dough well onto the bottom and sides of the tin, and pinch together or patch any gaps with dough trimmings. Don't trim off overhang. Place the tin on a baking sheet.

4 Fit a large sheet of foil into the pastry case, bringing it well up the sides. Fill with baking beans. Chill again for 20 minutes, whilst you preheat the oven to 180°C, Gas 4.

5 Bake the pastry case blind for 15 minutes. Remove the foil and beans, and bake for 5 more minutes. Trim the top of the pastry case level with the tin using a sharp knife, then set aside.

6 Place all the filling ingredients (except the rosemary-infused icing sugar) into a food processor and whiz until smooth and creamy. Spoon into the pastry case and level the top. Press the drained pears lightly on the surface in a circle, rounded side up. Bake for 35–40 minutes until the filling is firm and springs back when pressed on top. Cool until warm.

7 Serve in wedges dusted with rosemary-infused icing sugar.

Creamed sweet rice with autumn fruits

I make no excuses – this is a rich pudding, but worth every sweet, creamy mouthful. Serve it warm or cold (when it can be shaped into scoops or quenelles). The fruits add a good contrast in colour and flavour. **SERVES 4–6**

3 large red plums, stoned and sliced
1 large pear, peeled, cored and sliced
2 tablespoons icing sugar
100ml Stock Syrup (page 214) or apple juice
125g blackberries
1 vanilla pod
300ml creamy milk
300ml double cream
150g round-grain pudding rice
6 free-range egg yolks
150g caster sugar

1 Roast the fruits first. Get a clean non-stick frying pan really hot. Toss the plums and pear in the icing sugar, then cook briefly in the hot pan until they start to caramelise. This will take a couple of minutes. Remove and mix with the stock syrup or juice and the blackberries. Set aside to cool.
2 Slit the vanilla pod lengthways and, using the tip of a sharp knife, scrape out the seeds. Add these and the vanilla pod to the milk and cream in a heavy-based saucepan. Bring slowly to scalding point, when the liquid should start to rise up the sides of the pan.
3 Stir in the rice and return to the boil, stirring occasionally. Simmer gently, uncovered, for about 20 minutes until the rice is soft and most of the liquid absorbed.
4 Beat the egg yolks and caster sugar until creamy and smooth in a large heatproof bowl, placed on a damp cloth to hold it steady. Gradually mix in the hot rice, beating well. Return the lot to the pan and stir over a very gentle heat until it starts to thicken, about 5 minutes. Do not let the pudding overheat or it will curdle. Cool, stirring occasionally to stop a skin from forming. (We cool our pudding down rapidly over a bowl of crushed ice.)
5 Serve warm or cold, with the fruits and a little of their syrup spooned over.

winter

Surprisingly, winter can be a very good season for a variety of foods. Roots and brassicas are in prime condition, a lot of game is in high season, and fish from icy waters is plump and full of flavour. And now that air transport is so fast and efficient, we can obtain wonderful quality fresh fruits and vegetables from the southern hemisphere. So we can really have the best of both worlds.

Frosty, cold conditions may wilt some vegetables, but it seems to make certain hardy greens such as **cabbage** and sprouts more spriggy. My favourite cabbages are the Savoy and Chinese leaves. Obligingly, both remain crisp and fresh for several days in the fridge. The dark green, outer leaves of Savoy cabbage we use for wrapping up small, tightly packed balls of shredded braised oxtail or confit of duck. We also like to dry the large outer leaves, to use as a crisp garnish for sweetbreads. For this, the leaves are sautéed whole, then packed between metal baking sheets lined with non-stick baking parchment and baked at the lowest oven temperature for about 45 minutes. Chinese leaves are wonderful with braised and poached fish. We shred

the leaves finely into julienne strips, sauté them in butter with tips of thyme and then ladle in a little chicken stock just to moisten. This can be done ahead for reheating at the last moment.

Another very good leafy-cum-stalk vegetable for the winter months is **Swiss chard**, which I like to call by its French name *blette*. The two parts are prepared separately, with the leafy tops treated like spinach and the ribbed stalks like celery. They often need a light peeling before being cut into bâtons and sautéed. Chard is good with game. I also like to serve it with roasted bass with a vanilla-flavoured butter sauce (one of my first hallmark dishes at the Aubergine).

The Scots are very partial to **swedes** – I have many happy memories of my Mum's buttery golden purée – and they are popular in many other parts of the world. In France, however, swedes and other root vegetables were traditionally fed to the pigs. We may laugh at this, but I dare say the French could wag their fingers at us about our attitudes to celeriac and beetroot. The lightly sweet, slightly musky flavour of swede suits game birds such as pan-fried pigeons and roast guinea fowl as well as full-flavoured fish – I once tried it very successfully with a fillet of zander, a pike-perch type of fish popular in Europe. We cook swede in buttery stock first, then blend it until smooth and return the purée to the heat to dry off a little. Swede has enough body to stand on its own as a purée and doesn't need any potato.

The strange-looking **kohlrabi** may be a subject of curiosity for many of us, but take my word for it – the flavour cannot be matched by any other root

vegetable. It resembles a turnip, but is sweeter and more delicate. I think kohlrabi is best diced and sautéed in oil and butter before being braised with a little chicken stock until just tender. Like this it's good with light game, and it makes a light creamy soup too.

We tend to take large **'old' potatoes** for granted, tossing big bags into the supermarket trolley without looking at the label. But if you take time to check the variety, you can select potatoes with a fine flavour or those suitable for particular uses such as roasting or baking. I think it's worth paying a few extra pennies per kilo for the best – after all, a good potato is still the best value food. King Edwards, Desirée and Maris Piper are the 'aristos' of the spud world, being good for all uses. If you want to make mind-blowing mash, try baking them first, unpeeled, on a bed of rock salt. When soft, halve, scoop out the flesh and mash until smooth. Mix in half whipped cream and a good knob of best butter, and season nicely too – bland mash is a big disappointment. I like to serve chunky chips with steak tartare and – another example of the humble potato becoming a gourmet's delight – I make a simple creamy potato soup very special by stirring in fine shreds of black truffle.

A winter vegetable appreciated by both French and British chefs is **salsify** (see photograph on page 165). Home cooks are beginning to discover its joys too. The weird, dark, thin cigar-shaped roots do look a little uninviting, but peel them thinly and underneath you will find pale cream flesh that looks similar to white asparagus. Salsify has a tremendous flavour – robust and strong. Once peeled, it needs to be dunked into

lemony water because it browns quickly. After a blanch in boiling water, you can cut the stalks into thin lozenge shapes and sauté them in olive oil and butter until lightly browned. Salsify is fantastic with duck, veal and flat fish such as brill.

Although on sale almost all the year round, **leeks** are most often associated with winter dishes. In fact, leeks are best in the winter, before the inner cores harden, and we don't waste any part of them. The large outer leaves have a number of uses in our kitchen. The tougher ones act as wraps for bouquets garnis, while large inner leaves are turned into an attractive garnish: we shred them very finely and deep-fry them, then crisp them up in a low oven, ruffling through the shreds as they dry out to make them a bit 'bouffant'. We also confit bâtons of inner leek (and baby leeks too) in goose fat for about 8 minutes, then drain and grill them until crispy on the outside. Leeks marry well with most other savoury flavours, but I particularly like to sprinkle a pinch or two of crushed saffron strands over them as they braise in buttery stock or simmer in a leek soup. Whole baby leeks are great blanched and served with a lemon butter sauce.

If you are looking for unusual vegetable chips, then try leek leaves. Split open the white of a leek and cut the layers into large bite-size squares. Blanch to soften, then pat dry and brush each side with truffle oil. Dry them out in a very low oven until crisp. They'll be a sure talking point at any party, I promise.

Some vegetables have a foot in both camps – hot and cold. One of these is **chicory** (or endive, as the Continentals call it). Although most commonly used as a salad vegetable in the UK, in my kitchen we usually serve them cooked. They are best caramelised first in hot oil with a sprinkling of sugar, a good pinch of salt and a touch or two of Chinese five-spice. After this they can be moistened with fresh orange juice and a little chicken stock, covered with a butter paper and braised in a medium hot oven for about 15 minutes until tender but not soft. Braised chicory is great with fish, chicken and rabbit. I also like to make chicory 'fans' (make them like the fennel fans on page 136).

Where would any chef worth his or her salt be without **Puy lentils?** In France, where these lentils come from, they even have their own AOC. The uses for Puy lentils are almost endless. They're fantastic in soups, like our well-known cappuccino of lentils with langoustines; great mixed with a fine *brunoise* of carrots, celery and onions as a 'garnish' for lamb; and wonderful tossed with vinaigrette to serve with pigeon. We also use a fine purée of lentils as a thickener in soups and velouté sauces, although it does darken the colour somewhat. If you can't get Puy lentils, the larger greeny lentils from Canada are a reasonable substitute.

There is certainly an art to opening an **oyster**, and once you have mastered it you must then fine tune it with lots of practice! (The other two marks of a good chef in my book are filleting a sea bass and turning an artichoke.) You must never try to open an oyster from the side, it must be from the hinge at the top.

To shuck (or open) an oyster, wrap your hand in several layers of thick tea towel, and cup an oyster with the flat shell uppermost. Take a firm stubby knife with a good point (the classic oyster knife, if possible) and stick it in firmly, but not violently, at the hinge end. Wiggle it a little from side to side, and you should suddenly feel a 'give' as the hinge muscle is cut. Push the knife tip in a bit further and twist to lift up the shell. Inside is the oyster and juice. Be sure to save the juice. Slip the knife under the oyster to release the muscle, and that's it. A good oyster-opener leaves no bits of shell inside, although a novice is excused the occasional bit. The essence of opening is not speed but care. If we cook oysters at all, we just poach them in their own juice with a little nage and a couple of whole star anise. The smoky aromatic flavours blend sublimely. Native oysters (or Belons) are in season during the winter. They are more tricky to open than the commonly available Pacific oysters with their craggy shells.

There are many fishes more often associated with winter than warmer days. The first that comes to mind for most people is **cod**. Maybe that's because roasted and served with creamy mash, it's the ultimate comfort food. I associate cod with winter because that is when I used to go line fishing for it off a western Scottish beach with my dad. I think we were entrants in the White Horse whisky fishing championships. Anyway, although it is a great feeling to catch a big fish, from a cooking point of view, any fish over 5 kilos will be too flaky to hold together in the pan. The flakes are just too meaty, although the flavour is still fantastic. Instead, in the kitchen we like to cook smaller codlings around the 1.5–2 kilo size. Once filleted, the best way to cook cod is skin side down in a really hot pan, so the skin becomes very crispy. Then serve with a garlicky pomme purée or a

vinaigrette of Puy lentils. (Incidentally, when you cook cod skin, do check that the fine small scales have been rubbed off. It's not often the case.)

In today's quality restaurants, **brill** is becoming as popular as turbot. It's a strong fish, so can take a red wine marinade and full-bodied sauces made with chicken or veal stock, yet it still retains a fine tender texture when eaten. Brill are generally longer than turbots, but when they are small it is hard to tell them apart. If you buy a whole fish, turn it upside down and look for the 'oysters' by the jaw bone. Fillet them out with a sharp knife and pan-fry like scallops – they are a good cook's treat, or a garnish should you feel generous and want to share them. Brill bones make wonderful fish stock because they are quite gelatinous. Roast the brill bones first, as you would do meat bones, then cook in a red wine stock with strips of smoky bacon.

Red meats are a natural for winter dishes, and we are finding people are increasingly willing to try **venison**. Our venison is farmed on an estate in Aberdeenshire, where the deer are allowed to roam almost at will, so they are virtually free-range. The meat is hung for 2–3 weeks. After butchering, we marinate it in a neutral oil like groundnut with crushed juniper berries and fresh rosemary for a good 7 days. This opens up the muscle fibres and makes the meat really tender. We sometimes roast the loins and serve with rounds of fresh beetroot cooked fondant-style, in a little stock. Another favourite way of serving is with a garnish of chopped cabbage, turnip and carrot all braised together and then bound with a little cream. Slices of just pink venison are laid on top and nappéed

with a red wine sauce enriched with a bit of dark chocolate. The flavour intrigues our diners. A few fresh raspberries on top completes the elegant presentation.

Pork doesn't appear much on my menus, yet it is a meat that I think is perfect for serving home-cooked on chilly winter days. I love it with cabbage flavoured with a few pods of cardamom. If you find a butcher who still does his own cutting up, ask for the whole fillet of pork under the loin, the piggy equivalent of beef ribeye. The main way we use pork is **pig's trotters**. My three-star restaurant is on the site of what was Pierre Koffman's renowned Tante Claire. As I was once Pierre's head chef, this is an honour for me. Pierre's genius gave London many great dishes, but perhaps his best known were *pieds de cochon*, or stuffed pig's trotters. His most famous was a stuffing of sweetbreads and morels. My recipe for pig's trotters (which you will find on page 199) is really posh bacon and eggs. I serve it as an *amuse-gueule*. Trotters are very gelatinous and the thick, flavoursome braising liquid is a favourite staff lunch.

Another animal extremity that makes fine eating is **oxtail**. After an unnecessary (to my mind at least) ban of beef on the bone, we are now able to restore this classic casserole to pride of place on our winter menus. We stew oxtail gently in red wine with root vegetables, stock and a hint of spice. When the meat is very tender, it is pulled into shreds and bound in a ball with thin *crepine* or set in a terrine to be served in slices with a salad of lentils in mustard vinaigrette. Butchers sell oxtails as sets, with the vertebrae cut neatly into discs and bound with string. For a simpler serving, you could simply

cook them as a normal rich beef stew, but do try to take time to remove the meat from the bone before serving.

Two fruits brighten up the long winter days for me (not that we see much daylight in our kitchen). These are pineapples and citrus fruits. Large sweet **pineapples** come from the tropics and travel well. You can check their ripeness by pulling out a green leaf at the top – just a tug should do it. We use pineapple in *tarte Tatins*, compotes and sorbets, and to make terrific *tuiles*. For a light dessert, blend the flesh with a caramel sauce, and top with creamy yogurt and shavings of a fruit granita.

Oranges, lemons and limes are the fruits we most associate with winter, which is strange considering they don't grow in our cold climate. But they do travel and store well, and we are certainly grateful for them. Blood oranges and pink grapefruit are the two citrus fruits I like to feature when they come into season – **blood oranges** for their rich colour and startling flavour, and **pink grapefruit** because they break down into the prettiest little tear shapes. These we mix into a vinaigrette and serve with a warm salad of red mullet or poached Scottish lobster with fresh coriander.

One of our most refreshing desserts is a terrine of sliced citrus fruits with a tangy **lemon** sorbet. We also soak slices of lemon in stock syrup to make a sweet confit, and press them onto fillets of fish or sweetbreads before pan-roasting and serving with harissa-flavoured cous cous. The same can be done with **lime** slices, and cooked with pigeon breasts. Limes also feature as the tangy flavour in guacamole and in honey syrups for poaching all kinds of fruit.

Velouté of cauliflower
with a brunoise of scallops

This light cream soup has a velvety texture created by cooking tiny cauliflower florets in milk.
To finish, add some finely diced fresh scallops, which cook almost instantly in the hot liquid.
This soup is nicest served in elegant small teacups. **SERVES 4 AS A STARTER**

1 medium cauliflower
15g butter
250ml milk
200ml Light Chicken Stock (page 212)
   or Fish Stock (page 212)
100ml double cream
4 medium scallops, removed
   from their shells, without corals
tiny pinches of cayenne pepper
sea salt and freshly ground black pepper

1 Cut the cauliflower into florets. Discard the stalks (or save them for another use). Heat the butter in a saucepan, stir in the florets and gently sweat for up to 10 minutes, stirring occasionally.
2 Pour in the milk and add seasoning. Continue cooking gently for 5 minutes, then add the stock. Return to a simmer, partially cover the pan and cook until the florets are very soft, about 15 minutes. You should be able to press them gently against the side of the pan to crush. There is no need to blend in a processor.
3 Add the cream and cook for a few minutes longer. Check the seasoning.
4 Now, cut the scallops into small dice – what chefs call a *brunoise*. Divide this among four small soup cups or teacups. Season and dust with tiny pinches of cayenne.
5 Return the soup to the boil and pour over the scallops. Don't stir – the scallops should be a surprise! Eat soonest.

Creamy potato soup
with parsley Chantilly

This soup is made in a somewhat different way from the traditional 'sweat veg, add stock and blend to a purée' recipe. For a start, instead of boiling the potatoes, they are baked. The variety of potato is important. I recommend the golden-fleshed, well-flavoured Ratte because, despite its waxy texture, it has a lot of starch. Failing that, a Desirée or King Edward will do. I use a brown chicken stock to give the soup a country colour, and finish with stunning whipped cream and parsley floats. SERVES 4 AS A STARTER

about 50g curly-leaf parsley sprigs (no stalks)
3 cloves garlic
some rock salt, for baking
300g Ratte potatoes, washed
1 shallot, finely chopped
1 tablespoon olive oil
1 sprig fresh thyme
500ml Dark Chicken Stock (page 212)
100ml double cream
sea salt and freshly ground black pepper

1 Blanch the parsley sprigs in boiling water for 2 minutes, then drain in a colander and refresh under cold running water. Drain again and place in a clean tea towel. Wring the towel hard to extract the liquid. Purée the parsley in a food processor or, if you don't have one that can cope with such small quantities, chop the parsley very finely. Set aside.

2 Blanch the garlic in boiling water to cover for 30 seconds. Drain and blanch again. If you can bear it, repeat this a third time. This helps to remove the pungency of garlic, yet retains the flavour. Drain and crush the garlic.

3 Preheat the oven to 180°C, Gas 4. Sprinkle the bottom of a small roasting tin with rock salt and roll the wet potatoes in it. Bake for about 45 minutes until the flesh feels soft when pierced with a sharp knife. Cool until just comfortable enough to hold. (We wear rubber gloves for the next stage.) Peel the hot potatoes, then rub through a sieve with a ladle or push through a potato ricer. Set aside.

4 Sauté the shallot in the oil with the thyme for 5 minutes until soft. Mix in the potato and crushed garlic, and cook for a minute or two. Gradually stir in the stock as you would when making a risotto. This helps to keep the texture of the soup smooth and velvety. Season and bring to the boil. That's the soup made.

5 Now for the parsley *Chantilly*. Whip the cream until it holds its shape, season and fold in the parsley purée.

6 Serve the soup in bowls with the cream on top in soft dollops or more formal quenelles.

Fennel soup with baby clams

It is becoming easier to buy fresh baby clams from speciality fishmongers. Cook them like mussels until the shells open, then you can lift out the flesh. Save the juice for the soup – it adds to the flavour. **SERVES 4 AS A STARTER**

250g baby clams

100ml dry white wine

1 sprig fresh thyme

1 bay leaf

4 medium bulbs fennel

15g butter

1 tablespoon olive oil

1 onion, chopped

4 leaves fresh basil, chopped

2 tablespoons Pernod

1 litre Fish Stock (page 212)

200ml double cream

sea salt and freshly ground black pepper

Curry oil (optional)

3 tablespoons olive oil

1 teaspoon mild curry powder

1 First, cook the clams. Heat an empty saucepan until very hot, then tip in the clams, wine, thyme and bay leaf. Clamp on the lid and cook for about 5 minutes. Discard any clams that have not opened. Strain the juice and reserve. Pick out the meat from the shells and set aside.

2 Slice the base from the fennel bulbs and discard, then pull the segments apart. Slice them thinly lengthways into fine julienne strips.

3 Heat the butter and oil in a large saucepan and sauté the fennel strips and onion for about 10 minutes, stirring occasionally, until softened. Add the chopped basil and continue cooking for 2 minutes. Deglaze with the Pernod and cook for 1 minute, then pour in the fish stock and clam juice. Bring to the boil, season nicely and simmer for 15 minutes.

4 Meanwhile, for the optional curry oil garnish, heat the oil with the curry powder, stirring. When sizzling, remove from the heat and set aside.

5 Pass the soup through a fairly open sieve or colander so you keep some texture. Return to the pan, stir in the cream and check the seasoning. Bring back to the boil.

6 Divide the clams among four warmed soup bowls and ladle over the just boiling soup. This will be enough to reheat the cooked clams. Trickle over the curry oil, if using, and serve immediately.

Smoked haddock and mustard chowder

In Scotland they call a thick haddock and potato soup like this Cullen Skink, but I call this recipe a chowder so you all know what to expect. Do make sure you use natural undyed smoked haddock. My French training tempted me to add some coarsegrain French mustard, to celebrate the auld alliance. For a smart garnish, boil 4 quail's eggs for 2½ minutes, then peel and halve. Set on the soup just before serving. **SERVES 4 AS A STARTER**

1 large undyed Finnan haddock fillet, 400–500g
500ml milk
2 large waxy potatoes (such as Desirée),
　about 300g each
2 tablespoons olive oil
1 large shallot, chopped
100ml dry white wine
500ml Fish Stock (page 212)
90ml double cream
1 heaped tablespoon coarsegrain mustard
sea salt and freshly ground black pepper

1 Cut the haddock fillet in two or three pieces to fit into a large saucepan. Bring the milk to the boil in the saucepan, then slip in the 'haddie' fillet. Remove the pan from the heat and leave for about 10 minutes. By then the fish will feel firm when pressed.
2 Lift out the fish, then strain the milk and reserve. Skin and flake the fish whilst still warm. Set aside.
3 Peel the potatoes and cut into small dice. Heat the oil and sauté the potatoes with the shallot for about 10 minutes, stirring occasionally, until lightly coloured. Add the wine and cook until reduced right down, then pour in the stock and reserved milk. Season and bring to the boil, stirring once or twice. Simmer for 15 minutes until the potatoes feel just tender.
4 Whiz the mixture until smooth, either in the pan with a hand-held stick blender or decanted into a food processor or blender.
5 Return to the pan, if necessary, and blend in the cream. Briskly stir in the mustard and check the seasoning again. Gradually stir in the flaked haddie, reheat gently and serve.

Cabbage soup with rabbit shreds

We may not associate cabbage with soup, but it makes a nice homely first course or light meal with chunks of crusty bread. You need to cook the rabbit first until the flesh falls into tender shreds. I find cooking the legs slowly in goose fat is the best way. **SERVES 4 AS A STARTER OR LIGHT DISH**

about 300g goose fat (or a 340g can)
2 rabbit legs, about 250g each
1 small Savoy cabbage
6 large cloves garlic, peeled
40g butter
1 medium onion, chopped
50g smoked bacon, chopped
1 litre Dark Chicken Stock (page 212)
sea salt and freshly ground black pepper

1 Bring the goose fat to the boil in a saucepan, then drop in the rabbit legs. Turn the heat to its lowest setting and confit the rabbit for 30–40 minutes until the meat comes away from the bones easily.

2 Remove the rabbit legs from the fat and pat dry with kitchen paper towel. Heat the grill and, when hot, brown the meat on all sides. Cool, then pull the meat off the bones in shreds. Set aside.

3 Cut the cabbage in quarters, remove the core and shred the leaves finely. Blanch the garlic in boiling water three times, changing the water each time, to remove the pungency. Mash the cloves with a fork.

4 Melt the butter in a large saucepan and gently sauté the onion, bacon and garlic for about 5 minutes. Stir in the cabbage and cook for another 5 minutes until wilted. Pour in the stock and bring to the boil, then season. Simmer for 10 minutes.

5 Stir in the rabbit and simmer for a further 5–10 minutes. (If you have any to hand, you could add a handful or two of cooked Puy lentils or haricot beans with the rabbit.) Serve as it is, with bread.

Saffron-scented leek soup with pickled girolles

In this recipe for a favourite soup – leek and potato – there are two sophisticated twists. First, the vegetables are cooked with crushed saffron, and then the soup is served with some home-made pickled girolle mushrooms. **SERVES 4 AS A STARTER**

40g butter

1 tablespoon olive oil

1 large potato (such as Desirée), about 300g, peeled and diced

1 large leek (white and pale green part only), diced

1 medium onion, chopped

100ml dry white wine

2 good pinches of saffron strands, crushed

1 litre Light Chicken Stock (page 212)

90ml double cream

about 4 heaped tablespoons Pickled Girolles (page 213)

sea salt and freshly ground black pepper

1 Heat the butter and oil in a large saucepan and add the potato, leek and onion. Stir well and sauté gently for about 5 minutes until softened. Add the wine and boil until reduced right down, then stir in the crushed saffron and cook for a few more seconds. Pour in the stock, bring to the boil and season. Simmer gently for 12–15 minutes until the vegetables are softened.

2 Whiz in a food processor or blender until smooth, then press through a sieve into a clean pan, rubbing with the back of a ladle. Bring to the boil, then stir in the cream. Check the seasoning again.

3 To serve, spoon the pickled girolles in the centre of four warmed soup bowls and pour over the boiling soup. Serve hot.

Thai chicken soup

Nearly everyone loves chicken soup because it is warming, wholesome and very tasty. I love the flavours of Thai cooking and enjoy experimenting with the ingredients that are becoming increasingly easier to buy. They work well in a chicken soup. You need a nice clear and bright stock for this soup, so follow my tips. SERVES 4 AS A STARTER

1 litre Light Chicken Stock (page 212)
2 stalks fresh lemon grass, chopped
1 red, 1 yellow and 1 green pepper,
    finely diced
1 plump fresh red chilli, seeded
    and finely chopped
3 tablespoons olive or groundnut oil
4 baby pak choi
2 skinless, boneless chicken breasts,
    about 100g each, diced small

¼ teaspoon mild curry powder
a generous pinch of cayenne pepper
    or chilli powder
2 tablespoons coconut cream
leaves from 1 sprig fresh basil (ideally
    Thai holy basil, but Italian is fine)
sea salt and freshly ground black pepper

1 Tie up the lemon grass in a muslin bag (or use a clean J-Cloth). In a large saucepan, lightly sauté the diced peppers, fresh chilli and lemon grass bag in half the oil for about 5 minutes, stirring occasionally. Add the pak choi and continue cooking for 2 minutes until wilted. Set aside.
2 Heat the remaining oil in a clean non-stick frying pan and stir-fry the diced chicken with the curry powder and cayenne or chilli powder until just firm and a lovely golden brown colour, about 5 minutes. Remove and cool on kitchen paper towel.
3 Add the chicken to the peppers and chilli. Stir in the coconut cream and stock. Bring to the boil and check the seasoning, then tear in the basil leaves. Pull out the bag of lemon grass at the last minute.
4 Serve hot in warmed bowls, making sure each diner has a pak choi.

Note: Here are some helpful hints for making a clear stock. Before you begin, check that the chicken carcasses are well cleaned and free of any blood spots – it is best to rinse them under a cold tap. Simmer the stock rather than boil and, when cooked, allow it to stand for a good 15 minutes so the solids settle to the bottom of the pan. Then very gently pour through a muslin-lined sieve, leaving the solids and 'debris' behind.

Salad of foie gras, green beans and artichokes

Fresh foie gras – those pale rose-pink lobes – is best cooked very gently and lightly in goose fat, a process the French call 'confit'. We use duck foie gras and serve it cold for a starter, with a crisp salad dressed with truffle cream vinaigrette. Sourdough pain Poilâne or brioche toast are traditional accompaniments. (I must confess that I have enjoyed the occasional slice on toast in front of the TV on a Saturday afternoon – my idea of heaven: foie gras and football!) Serve with a glass of luscious Sauternes or fruity Dom Perignon. SERVES 6 AS A STARTER

1 lobe fresh foie gras, 400–450g
2 x 340g cans goose fat
6 medium globe artichokes
a squeeze of lemon juice
150g thin green beans, topped and tailed
sea salt and freshly ground black pepper

Vinaigrette
1 tablespoon sherry vinegar
80ml groundnut oil
1 tablespoon extra virgin olive oil
1 tablespoon truffle oil
2 tablespoons double cream
1 teaspoon finely chopped or grated truffle
$^1/_2$ teaspoon sea salt

1 Prepare the foie gras (see page 86). Season the insides and push together again to reshape.
2 Heat a large non-stick frying pan and, when you can feel a good heat rising, add the foie gras, pressing it down well onto the hot pan. Sear and brown it quickly all over. (You may find turning it a bit slippy. Your hands are best, but wrap them in a clean tea towel so your fingers aren't burnt.) Don't brown the outside for too long, just a few seconds, or you will find the foie gras disappears before your very eyes. Remove it from the pan. (A lot of fat will come from the foie gras, which shouldn't be discarded. Strain it off and use to fry eggs or mushrooms.)
3 Heat the goose fat in a deep saucepan that will just hold the lobe of foie gras. Using a sugar thermometer, keep the heat of the fat to just 54°C (that's the temperature for making yogurt). You may find it useful to use a metal heat diffuser.
4 Slip the foie gras into the fat, making sure it is submerged completely, and confit for 5 minutes at the lowest temperature possible. Lift it out onto a wire rack, and drain and cool for 20 minutes. Then wrap tightly in a double thickness of cling film and chill. It can be kept in the fridge for up to 4 days – foie gras matures as it stores.
5 Whisk together the ingredients for the vinaigrette. (This makes 150ml, so what isn't used in the salad can be kept in a large screw-topped jar in the fridge.)
6 Cut the stalks from the artichokes, pull off the leaves and scoop out the hairy choke (see photographs of this technique on page 216). Cut the meaty heart into strips. Cook in boiling water with the lemon juice for 2 minutes. Drain and pat dry. Blanch the green beans in boiling salted water for 2 minutes, then drain and refresh under cold running water.
7 Season the beans and artichokes, and dress with 3–4 tablespoons of the truffle cream vinaigrette. Divide among four plates. Top with slivers of foie gras, sliced thinly with a sharp knife dipped in hot water.

Salt cod pâté with cherry tomato dressing

Salt cod is a popular ingredient in many parts of the world, from the Mediterranean to the West Indies (for reasons historical). Salting the flesh of cod concentrates the flavour and firms the texture. The Spanish, Portuguese and French all have wonderful recipes for flaked salt cod and creamed potato, shaping the mixture into fritters or brandades. *Salt cod can be bought in various grades and strengths, but it is easy to make yourself and requires only 24 hours advance salting. So, let's start with that. Incidentally, freshly made salt cod has many other uses, so you might consider making double the quantity. Once lightly poached and flaked, you can use it in fish cakes or serve it with a cream of parsley sauce. The pâté is a great party dish, and the cherry tomato dressing can also be used as a light dip for crudités and croûtes cut from ficelles (small baguettes).* **SERVES 4 AS A STARTER**

300g fillet of cod
60g sea salt flakes
a few fresh parsley stalks, twisted
2 good pinches of curry powder
1 tablespoon olive oil
1 medium waxy potato (such as
   Maris Piper), peeled and diced
300ml milk
1 fat clove garlic, crushed
1 tablespoon chopped fresh parsley
100ml double cream
sea salt and freshly ground black pepper

Dressing
200g naturally ripened
   cherry tomatoes
$\frac{1}{2}$ teaspoon caster sugar
100ml groundnut or olive oil,
   plus extra for drizzling
1 tablespoon Dijon mustard

1 Lay the cod in a shallow dish and sprinkle over the salt and parsley stalks. Cover the fish with cling film, then press a heavy plate on top. Chill for 24 hours, turning once, by which time you will find liquid oozing out and the fish firmed up.

2 Drain, rinse in cold water and pat dry. Discard the parsley stalks. The cod fillet should now weigh about 200g.

3 Cut the cod into large chunks and dust with curry powder. Heat the oil in a non-stick frying pan and sauté the cod until a good golden brown and quite firm. It is best overcooked slightly. Drain, cool and flake. Set aside.

4 Cook the potato in the milk with the crushed garlic and seasoning. Drain well, reserving some of the milk. Blend to a purée in a food processor (one of the few times when I do allow this!). If the mixture is a bit thick, trickle in some of the saved milk.

5 Cool the potato, then mix in the flaked cod and parsley. Whip the cream until it holds soft peaks. Fold into the cod mixture. Check the seasoning. Chill the mixture in a bowl should you wish to shape it into quenelles, or just press into ramekins and mark the top with the tip of a knife or tines of a fork.

6 For the dressing, whiz the tomatoes to a purée in a food processor. Press the purée through a sieve into a bowl, rubbing with the back of a ladle. Mix in the sugar, oil, mustard and seasoning. That's it. There is no need for any vinegar as the tomatoes are acid enough. (This makes 200ml, which leaves plenty of extra dressing to serve with crudités.)

7 If serving the pâté in a bowl or ramekins, you can make a hollow in the centre and fill with some of the fresh tomato dressing, or trickle it over the top with a little extra olive oil. Another suggestion is to spread the pâté thickly on croûtes, sprinkle with freshly grated Parmesan and grill until lightly browned.

Seafood in a nage with carrot spaghetti

This is my version of a plat de fruits de mer *– a glorious collection of favourite seafood served in a light aromatic vegetable broth scented with star anise. It is served with a thin 'spaghetti' of carrots, which can be cut on a razor-sharp mandolin or food processor attachment.*

SERVES 4 AS A MAIN DISH

2 carrots
70g butter
500ml Vegetable Nage (page 212),
   plus 3 tablespoons
3 star anise
150g baby clams in shells
3 tablespoons dry white wine
8 rock oysters
4 large scallops, removed from
   their shells, without corals
2 tablespoons double cream
a good squeeze of lemon juice
1 heaped tablespoon shredded fresh basil
sea salt and freshly ground black pepper

1 First, cut the carrots into long thin 'spaghetti' using a mandolin, Japanese slicer or an equivalent slicer blade on a food processor. Bring the butter and the 3 tablespoons of nage to the boil. Stir in the carrot spaghetti, season and cover. Cook for 1 minute, then set aside.

2 Heat the rest of the nage until boiling. Add the star anise, then remove from the heat and infuse for 10 minutes. Discard the anise.

3 Heat a large saucepan and, when hot, add the clams and wine. Clamp on the lid and cook for 3–5 minutes, shaking the pan occasionally, until the shells open. Discard any clams whose shells remain steadfastly shut. Pick the meat from the shells and set aside. Strain and save the juice.

4 Open the oysters, saving the juice (if the fishmonger does this, be sure to ask him to save the juice). Cut each scallop horizontally in three.

5 Reheat the nage and slip in the slices of scallops. Heat on a bare simmer, then add the oysters and cook for 1 minute. Finally, drop in the shelled clams. Stir in the saved juices too. Check the seasoning, and stir in the cream, lemon juice and basil.

6 As soon as everything is hot, divide the seafood among four soup bowls and ladle over the hot stock. Top with the carrot spaghetti and serve.

Brill in red wine with beurre rouge

You may find it strange cooking white fish in red wine, but it works really well and looks so attractive when you cut into the fillet. The sauce, called a beurre rouge, *is made by reducing the liquor down and whisking in butter. Vegetable accompaniments include potato purée, butter-glazed grelot onions (or baby shallots) and salsify.* **SERVES 4 AS A MAIN DISH**

500g potatoes (such as Desirée)
5 tablespoons double cream
150g butter, plus a good knob
150g salsify
a good squeeze of lemon juice
3 tablespoons olive oil
12 grelot onions, peeled
1 large shallot, finely chopped
500ml red wine
500ml Fish Stock (page 212)
4 fillets of brill, about 150g each
1 tablespoon chopped fresh parsley
sea salt and fresh ground black pepper

1 Cook the potatoes, in their skins, in boiling salted water for 12–15 minutes until tender, then drain. Peel whilst hot (wear rubber gloves), then mash or press through a potato ricer back into the pan. Heat for a minute or two, then beat in 3 tablespoons of the cream and 25g of the butter until thick and creamy. Season and set aside.

2 Peel the salsify with a swivel peeler, then rinse well and slice diagonally into thin bâtons. Blanch in boiling water with the lemon juice for 2 minutes, then drain and cool.

3 Heat 2 tablespoons of the oil and, when hot, sauté the onions for about 5 minutes, turning frequently. Pat the salsify dry, then add to the pan with the knob of butter. Cook for a few more minutes until nicely coloured. Set aside and keep warm.

4 Heat the remaining oil in a medium saucepan and gently sauté the shallot for 5 minutes. Pour in the wine and stock, and bring to a gentle simmer.

5 Trim the brill fillets to neaten, and season them. Slip into the hot liquid. Poach the fish for 3–4 minutes until just tender. Do not overcook. Remove the fish with a fish slice and keep warm.

6 Strain the fish liquor through a fine sieve, then return to the pan. Boil rapidly until reduced by two-thirds, then stir in the remaining cream and some seasoning. Bring back to a gentle boil, then, on a low heat, whisk in the remaining butter, cut in small cubes, adding them one or two at a time. The sauce will thicken slightly and become glossy. Watch carefully that it doesn't 'split'.

7 Reheat the potato purée and divide among four warmed plates. Sit a brill fillet on top of each mound of potatoes and arrange the glazed vegetables around. Nappé with the *beurre rouge*, sprinkle with parsley and serve.

Cod with crispy potatoes and mustard lentils

Fish, potatoes and pulses are natural partners – think of fish and chips with mushy peas. This is a more sophisticated variation, using the waxy Belle Fontaine potatoes and dainty Puy lentils. A terrific light winter main course. **SERVES 4 AS A MAIN DISH**

400g even-sized Belle Fontaine
   potatoes, scrubbed
4 tablespoons olive oil
4 fillets of cod, about 125g each, with skin
100g Puy lentils
1 carrot
½ small onion
1 small stick celery

15g butter
1 shallot, finely chopped
1 tablespoon capers, rinsed and patted dry
2 tablespoons Classic Vinaigrette (page 213)
   mixed with 1 teaspoon Dijon mustard
1 tablespoon chopped fresh chives
sea salt and freshly ground black pepper

1 Cook the potatoes in boiling salted water for about 12 minutes until just tender. Drain and cool until you can handle them – they are best peeled hot (we put on rubber gloves). Cut into neat dice and toss with 1 tablespoon of the oil. Spread out on a tray, season and let the potatoes absorb the oil as they cool.

2 Season the skin side of the cod with salt, rubbing it in nicely. Leave for half an hour. This helps to dry out the skin.

3 Place the lentils in a saucepan with the carrot, onion and celery. Cover with cold water and bring to the boil. Simmer for about 15 minutes or until just cooked. Do not overcook or the lentils will break down. Drain immediately and discard the vegetables. Spread the lentils on a tray to cool. This stops them cooking further.

4 When ready to cook, heat 1 tablespoon of the oil with the butter in a frying pan, and gently sauté the shallot for about 5 minutes. Scoop out the shallot and reserve. Add another tablespoon of oil to the pan, raise the heat and tip in the diced potato. Cook until nicely golden brown, turning as necessary. Remove, mix with the shallot and capers, and keep warm.

5 Wipe out the pan and heat the remaining tablespoon of oil in it. When hot, add the fish, skin side down. Cook until the skin crisps up nicely (make sure the heat isn't too high or the skin will burn). I always cook my cod for 90% of the total time on the skin side, then flip over just to brown the other side lightly. Cooking time depends on the thickness of the fillet, but is about 5 minutes in all. Check if the fish is cooked by pressing with the back of a fork. It should be lightly springy.

6 Reheat the lentils briefly in a saucepan, season and stir in the vinaigrette and chives. Sit a cod fillet on each of four warmed plates, and spoon over the lentils and then the potatoes. Serve hot.

Baby red mullets with choucroute and rhubarb

Little red mullets are filleted into a butterfly shape, then marinated and pan-fried. These are served on a salad that might make you gasp – choucroute with celery and rhubarb dressed with pink grapefruit vinaigrette. It has to be tried to be believed! Baby new potatoes and blanched spinach are good accompaniments. **SERVES 4 AS A MAIN DISH**

4 small red mullets, about 200g each
3 tablespoons olive oil
2 pinches of saffron strands, crushed
4 sticks pink rhubarb, trimmed
4 inner sticks of celery, trimmed
100g choucroute (sauerkraut)
    from a jar, rinsed in cold water

150ml Vegetable Nage (page 212)
15g butter
1 pink grapefruit
5 tablespoons Classic Vinaigrette (page 213)
leaves from 2 sprigs fresh coriander, shredded
sea salt and freshly ground black pepper

1 Cut the heads from the mullets, then, using kitchen scissors, cut along the belly of each fish and gut. Wash the cavity well under cold running water, rubbing away any blood spots. Lay the fish on a board and slit down to the tail end. Using the tip of a sharp filleting knife, loosen the backbone and finer bones from the flesh on both sides, then snip the bones carefully from the skin and discard. You want to fillet the fish, keeping the two sides joined together to form a butterfly shape. (See photographs of this technique on page 217.)

2 Pat the fish dry. Brush both sides with 1 tablespoon of the olive oil. Crush the saffron over the pink skins and rub in. Chill uncovered for 2 hours.

3 Meanwhile, make the choucroute salad. Cut the rhubarb and celery into thin bâtons 4cm long. Sweat the choucroute in the rest of the oil for 3 minutes, then add the rhubarb and celery. Cook for a further 2 minutes. Pour in the nage and seasoning. Dot with the butter and place a butter paper on top. Turn the heat right down and simmer very gently for 10 minutes, basting once or twice.

4 Meanwhile, peel the grapefruit, removing all white pith, and cut out the segments from the membrane. Break up the grapefruit segments in a bowl with a fork into little pink 'tears'. Mix with the vinaigrette.

5 Remove the choucroute from the heat and mix in half the grapefruit vinaigrette. Check the seasoning. Allow to cool to room temperature, then toss in the coriander.

6 When ready to serve, heat a large non-stick frying pan and, when hot, fry the mullets for 3–4 minutes on the skin side until crisp. Flip them over carefully and cook briefly on the other side. Do not overcook, as the fish are small and delicate.

7 Divide the salad among four plates and place a pretty fish on top of each. Glaze with the rest of the grapefruit vinaigrette and serve.

Dorade royale with a ragoût of blette

Dorades are confusing fish, or rather it is the variety of names attached to them that confuses. In French they are daurade, *and in English they're also known as breams. The dorade royale is the black bream – just one of the many varieties. Popular in many Mediterranean countries, dorades/breams are now being farmed, which makes them more available, although wild fish still has the edge on flavour and texture.* Blette *is the French name for Swiss chard. The stalks and leaves are cooked separately, and then combined in a creamy grain mustard sauce.*

SERVES 4 AS A MAIN DISH

4 fillets of dorade royale,
   about 125g each, skin on
1 fat clove garlic, halved
3 tablespoons olive oil
500g Swiss chard
juice of 1 lemon
25g butter
100ml Dark Chicken Stock (page 212)
100ml double cream
1 tablespoon Pommery coarsegrain mustard
1 teaspoon fresh thyme leaves
sea salt and freshly ground black pepper

1 Rub the fish flesh with the cut clove of garlic, then brush with half of the olive oil. Set aside to marinate in the fridge whilst you prepare the chard.

2 Wash the chard well and pat dry. Cut off the leaves and tear up into bite-size pieces. Using a swivel vegetable peeler, peel the stalks lightly, then cut into 4cm long bâtons. As you cut, drop them into cold water acidulated with the lemon juice, to prevent them from turning brown. When ready to cook, drain and pat dry.

3 Sweat the chard bâtons in the butter for 4–5 minutes, then add the stock and seasoning. Cook for another 4 minutes, then stir in the cream and mustard. Keep warm.

4 Meanwhile, blanch the chard leaves in a little boiling salted water for 2 minutes. Drain, refresh under cold running water and drain well again. Stir into the creamy ragoût of chard bâtons and check the seasoning.

5 When ready to serve, heat a large non-stick pan and add a trickle of oil if you wish. Cook the fish fillets skin side down for 3–4 minutes. Season the top as they cook, sprinkle over the thyme leaves and baste once or twice with the pan juices. Turn the fillets carefully and cook the other side for a minute or until the fish feels just cooked. Do not overcook.

6 Spoon the ragoût into four shallow soup plates and sit a fish fillet on top of each. Serve hot.

A quick casserole of pigeon

Casseroles don't have to be cooked long and slow. This one simmers diced winter vegetables in a rich red wine stock and is served with pan-fried breasts of wood pigeon. There's not much meat on a wood pigeon, so I only bother to cook the breasts, serving two for each portion.

SERVES 4 AS A MAIN DISH

4 nice fat wood pigeons

about 150g salsify

1 small celeriac

1 small swede

2 medium parsnips

4 small red onions or 8 baby ones, peeled

4 tablespoons olive oil

1 sprig fresh rosemary

1 bay leaf

300ml red wine

1 teaspoon tomato purée

1 teaspoon truffle oil

1 litre Dark Chicken Stock (page 212)

50g mousserons or baby button mushrooms

sea salt and freshly ground black pepper

1 Cut the breasts from the pigeons, so you have two breasts per person. Discard the carcasses (or use to make stock). Set aside.

2 Peel the salsify, celeriac, swede and parsnips, and cut into large dice. If using small rather than baby onions, cut each in half. Heat 1½ tablespoons of the oil in a large pan and tip in all the vegetables including the onions. Toss in the herbs too. Sweat the vegetables for a good 10 minutes so they become nicely coloured.

3 Meanwhile, boil the wine right down until reduced to around 100ml. Stir the tomato purée and the truffle oil into the vegetables, then stir in the wine, stock and some seasoning. Simmer uncovered until the vegetables are just tender, 10–12 minutes. The vegetables should have become wine-stained and the liquid reduced right down.

4 For the pigeons, heat 1½ tablespoons of the remaining oil in a large frying pan. Season the breasts and quickly fry, skin side down first, for a total of about 6 minutes. The breasts should be lightly springy when pressed and still a little pink inside.

5 Meanwhile, quickly sauté the mousserons in the remaining 1 tablespoon of oil.

6 Divide all the vegetables among four warmed shallow soup plates. Set the pigeon breasts on top, season and serve.

Woodcock with caramelised parsnips and chocolate sauce

Woodcocks are regarded by aficionados to be the most delicious of all game birds. They are only lightly hung, just a day or two. Dainty in size, with delicate skin, they cook very quickly. The traditional method is to cook them with their heads tucked under their wings and with their innards intact. I like to cook woodcock in two stages and then serve them with thick bâtons of parsnips cooked in a caramel and balsamic vinegar glaze, and with a rich red wine sauce flavoured with just a bit of dark chocolate. It is an elegant dish reminiscent of the best in country house cooking. Be sure to buy woodcock from licensed game dealers – they have a short season (November to January). **SERVES 4 AS A MAIN DISH**

4 woodcocks
4 tablespoons clarified butter
25g cold butter, cut in cubes
sea salt and freshly ground black pepper

Sauce
300ml red wine
1 large shallot, finely chopped
1 tablespoon olive oil
$1/4$ teaspoon Chinese five-spice powder
6 black peppercorns
1 sprig fresh thyme
1 small bay leaf
2 teaspoons sherry vinegar
500ml Dark Chicken Stock (page 212)
25g dark chocolate, with at least
   60% cocoa solids

Parsnips
6 medium dumpy parsnips
4 tablespoons sugar
$1/2$ teaspoon fine sea salt
3 tablespoons olive oil
15g butter
1 tablespoon clear honey
1 tablespoon aged balsamic vinegar
150ml Dark Chicken Stock (page 212)

1 Make the sauce first. Boil the wine until reduced by half. In another pan, sauté the shallot in the oil for 5 minutes. Add the spice, peppercorns and herbs. Cook for 1 minute, then deglaze with the vinegar. Stir in the reduced wine and then the stock. Season, bring to the boil and cook on a medium heat until reduced by half. Strain and reserve in the same saucepan.

2 Now, prepare the parsnips. Peel and trim the tops and tails. Cut in half widthways. Slice down the parsnips around the central core like thick chips. Discard the cores. Toss the parsnip chips in a mixture of the sugar and salt.

3 Heat the oil and butter in a large shallow pan and fry the parsnips until they start to caramelise, turning frequently until nicely golden brown. Stir in the honey and carry on cooking until the parsnips soften, about 5 minutes. Deglaze with the balsamic vinegar for a minute or two, then pour in the stock gradually. Don't add it all at once or you will dissolve the caramel. Add it in small slurps and let one lot be absorbed before you add another, like adding the stock when making a risotto. You should have a nice syrupy sauce at the end. Remove the parsnips from the heat and keep warm.

4 When you are ready to cook the woodcocks, preheat the oven to 200°C, Gas 6. Heat 1 tablespoon of the clarified butter in a frying pan. Wrap your hand in a clean tea towel and put one bird into the pan, breast side down, pressing it into the hot fat. Brown it, then turn to brown the other breast. Sear the rest of the bird too if you like, although you only need the breasts for this dish. Remove the woodcock, and repeat with the remaining birds and clarified butter, browning each individually.

5 Place the birds in a small roasting tin, standing up on their bottoms. Dot with knobs of cold butter. Heat the tin on the hob until the butter starts to foam, then trickle this butter over the breasts of the birds. Put into the oven and roast for about 10 minutes. The meat will be very pink.

6 Remove and allow to rest until cool enough to handle, then take off each breast in one piece using a sharp boning knife. Cut off the legs too if you wish, although the meat on them doesn't amount to much.

7 Return the breasts (and legs if using) to the tin, spoon over the pan juices and cover with a butter paper. Put back into the oven at the same temperature and cook for 3–4 more minutes.

8 Reheat the parsnips and divide among four warmed plates. Return the sauce to the boil, then off the heat stir in the chocolate until it melts. Check the seasoning. Serve two breasts each on the parsnips and nappé with the sauce.

Gressingham duck with chicory tarts

Gressingham ducks are one of my favourite things, full of flavour, with a skin that crisps nicely – as long as you score the skin closely and evenly. The chicory tarts are an unusual accompaniment. They take a wee while to put together, but they are not difficult. You will need tartlet tins or large muffin tins for this, 8–10cm diameter and 2–3cm deep. **SERVES 4 AS A MAIN DISH**

250g Puff Pastry (page 214)

4 medium heads chicory

30g light soft brown sugar

50g butter, plus a good knob

2 tablespoons balsamic vinegar

1 carrot, diced

¼ celeriac, diced

½ small Savoy cabbage, finely shredded

1 tablespoon olive oil

75g smoked lean bacon, cut in small cubes

4 breasts of Gressingham duck, about 175g each

1 tablespoon clear honey

2 whole cloves

sea salt and freshly ground black pepper

1 Roll out the pastry to 5mm thickness. Cut out four rounds a good 3cm larger than the diameter of your tartlet tins, that is 11–13 cm. Prick the bases lightly and chill to rest. Preheat the oven to 200°C, Gas 6.

2 Using a thin sharp knife, tunnel-core the chicory to remove as much of the hard core as possible, yet still keeping the leaves together. Cut the chicory across so you have the dumpy section from each about 3cm tall. Set aside. (Use the leafy tops in salads.)

3 In a small saucepan, dissolve the sugar in a small sprinkling of water, then add the butter. Melt it, then boil for a minute or so. Mix in the vinegar. Pour this into the tartlet tins. Season the chicory sections, then press one down into the caramel in each tin, cored side up. (See photographs of this technique on page 218.)

4 Fit the pastry discs on top, tucking the edges down inside the tin around the sides. Bake for 12–15 minutes until the pastry is golden brown and crisp. Once or twice during baking, carefully tip out any juices from the tins. The chicory will soften and take on a delicious caramelised flavour. Remove and allow to cool a bit whilst you make the rest of the dish.

5 Blanch the carrot and celeriac in boiling salted water for 3–4 minutes. Add the cabbage and cook for a further 2 minutes. Drain and refresh under cold running water. Wipe out the pan, heat the oil in it and fry the bacon lardons for about 5 minutes, stirring once or twice. Set the pan aside.

6 Trim the duck breasts neatly, then score the skin, taking care not to cut through the fat as well. The closer the scoring lines are together, the crisper the cooked skin. Heat a non-stick heavy-based frying pan and, when hot, put in the duck breasts, skin side down. Cook for a few moments to brown. Fat will seep out. Tip this away so it does not burn. Turn the breasts and brown the flesh side. Season as they cook. Turn once more and baste the flesh side a few times with the pan juices. Cook for a total of 8–10 minutes. Duck is best served slightly pink and juicy.

7 Remove the duck breasts from the pan and keep warm, saving the juices that seep out. Drain off the excess fat from the pan, but hold back the meaty juices. Add the honey and cloves, then

return the duck breasts with their juices, and glaze with the honey mixture. Give the skin side one more turn in the pan to crisp it, then remove the breasts and leave to rest briefly.

8 Meanwhile, reheat the bacon lardons, then add the knob of butter and return the cabbage mixture to the pan. Stir gently until piping hot. Check the seasoning, then spoon in mounds in the centre of four warmed plates. Sit the duck breasts on top (cut into slices diagonally if you like) and trickle over the pan juices. Carefully turn out the chicory tarts, loosening them with a table knife if necessary, and place one on each plate. Using a thin spoon handle or table knife, gently separate the chicory leaves to give a rose effect. Serve immediately.

Loin of pork with choucroute and mustard cream sauce

Pork is at its best in the middle of winter. Do choose outdoor-reared pork, because it has so much more flavour than the alternative. Ask the butcher for a best end of the loin, with rind that has been well scored so it will crisp to light crackling. Talking of which, if you want nice crisp crackling, then follow my suggestion to sear the rind first in a hot pan before roasting.
With the pork, I like to serve choucroute cooked in the Alsace style with crispy lardons of bacon.

SERVES 4 AS A MAIN DISH

1 boned pork loin joint, about 1kg
500g jar choucroute (sauerkraut)
2 tablespoons olive oil
1 onion, sliced
75g smoked lean bacon, cut in small cubes
800ml Dark Chicken Stock (page 212)
150ml double cream
1 tablespoon coarsegrain mustard
sea salt and freshly ground black pepper

1 Preheat the oven to 200°C, Gas 6. Heat a large frying pan on the hob until you can feel a strong heat rising. Put the joint of pork in the pan, rind down, and press onto the hot pan (you might want to wrap your hand in a cloth to protect it). This will start the crackling crisping. Turn the joint and brown the rest of it.

2 Transfer the joint to a roasting tin, placing it rind side up, and sprinkle with sea salt. Roast for 30 minutes, then turn the temperature down to 180°C, Gas 4. Roast for a further 30 minutes. Do not baste.

3 Meanwhile, rinse the choucroute in cold water and drain well. Heat 1 tablespoon of oil in a large saucepan and gently sauté the onion for 5 minutes until lightly coloured. Stir in the bacon and continue cooking for about 3 minutes until crisp. Mix in the choucroute, and stir in 500ml of the stock and freshly ground pepper. Bring to the boil, then cover and simmer very gently for about 20 minutes.

4 Meanwhile, boil the remaining stock until reduced by half. Tip out of the pan and save, and pour the cream into the pan. Bring the cream to the boil, slowly, then mix in the reduced stock plus the mustard. Check the seasoning and keep the sauce warm.

5 When the pork is nearing the end of its cooking, pierce the thickest section with a thin skewer. Clear juices should run out. If not, cook it for longer until the juices are clear. The pork should feel just firm when pressed, but not rock solid. Remove from the oven and allow to rest for about 10 minutes whilst you reheat the sauce and divide the choucroute among four warmed plates.

6 Carve the pork into fairly thick slices, and break up the crackling into pieces. Place on top of the choucroute, and nappé with the sauce. Sheer rustic pleasure.

Veal chops with a cream of winter vegetables

Veal is not overly popular in Britain, which is a shame because it has such a great flavour and is so versatile. You can serve it simply roasted or cooked with a sauce – a cream sauce as in a blanquette de veau *or a punchy tomato-based sauce such as in* osso bucco. *This is a nice recipe for a mid-week dinner – meat and vegetables all in one, celeriac and cabbage served with blanched baby spinach.* **SERVES 4 AS A MAIN DISH**

4 veal loin chops, about 200g each
4 tablespoons olive oil
1 teaspoon chopped fresh rosemary
8–12 baby onions
150g celeriac
25g butter, plus a knob
200g baby leaf spinach
1 tablespoon Dijon mustard
200ml double cream
sea salt and freshly ground black pepper

1 Trim the chops, then place flat on a board. Using a rolling pin, beat the loin lightly to flatten slightly. Brush both sides of each chop with a little olive oil and sprinkle with rosemary. Leave to marinate for about 2 hours.

2 Meanwhile, blanch the onions in boiling water for 30 seconds. Drain and rinse in cold water. The skins should slip off easily. Heat 1 tablespoon of oil in a small pan and sauté the onions for 5–7 minutes until golden brown. Remove with a slotted spoon and set aside.

3 Peel the celeriac and cut into dice. Heat the remaining oil and the butter in the same pan and sauté the celeriac for about 5 minutes, turning once or twice. Season nicely and return the onions to the pan. Set aside.

4 Blanch the spinach in boiling water for 1 minute, then drain and refresh under a cold running tap. Drain well again and press out as much water as possible. (In my kitchen, I squeeze the leaves in a clean tea towel.)

5 Stir the mustard and cream into the celeriac and onions, and bring slowly to the boil. Check the seasoning. Keep warm.

6 Now for the veal. Heat a heavy-based non-stick frying pan and, when hot, put in the veal chops. Season as they cook, allowing 3–4 minutes on each side. Baste once or twice with any pan juices or any leftover marinade.

7 Reheat the spinach with the knob of butter. Divide the celeriac and onions among four warmed plates, sit the chops on top and spoon the spinach around. Serve hot.

Escalope of veal with fondant kohlrabi and baby globe artichokes

Winter is a good season for using baby globe artichokes. These are so young the chokes have not yet formed, so can be cooked and eaten whole. Winter is also the time for kohlrabi, with its intriguing turnip-like flavour. If you take time to prepare special vegetable dishes, then it makes sense to serve with a quick-cook cut of meat. My favourite is a slice of 'cushion' of veal (from the top rump), which is called an escalope, although a thin fillet of lamb or pork would do nicely too.

SERVES 4 AS A MAIN DISH

4 baby globe artichokes

juice of ½ lemon

1 medium kohlrabi, about 500g

25g butter

1 tablespoon olive oil

150ml Light Chicken Stock (page 212)

4 escalopes of veal, about 100g each

3 tablespoons plain flour

3 tablespoons clarified butter

2 teaspoons chopped fresh chervil

2 teaspoons chopped fresh parsley

2 teaspoons chopped fresh chives

sea salt and freshly ground black pepper

1 First prepare the artichokes. Trim the tips of the leaves and snap off the stalks. Drop into a pan of boiling water with half the lemon juice. Cook for 5 minutes, then drain upside down in a colander. Cool.

2 Peel the kohlrabi and slice into 1.5cm thick rounds. Heat half the butter and the oil in a sauteuse or shallow saucepan. Fry the kohlrabi slices quickly on both sides to brown nicely, then season and pour in the stock. Add half of the remaining butter to the pan and cover with a butter paper. Simmer gently until the stock has evaporated and the slices have softened, 10–12 minutes. Do not turn them. Leave in the pan, but remove from the heat.

3 Now for the veal. Place one of the escalopes between non-stick baking parchment and beat lightly with the flat of a metal cleaver or rolling pin. Don't whack the life out of the meat – just a light battening to flatten and tenderise. Repeat with the other escalopes. Season the flour and toss the veal in it, shaking off any excess.

4 Heat the clarified butter in a heavy-based non-stick frying pan and lay in the veal. Fry quickly for a minute to sear, then slip in the remaining bit of butter. When it froths, turn the veal over. Baste with the frothing butter and cook for 1–2 minutes until the meat feels just firm. Don't overcook. Toss in the chopped herbs, season lightly and squeeze over the remaining lemon juice.

5 Serve the veal on warmed plates. Reheat the artichokes (in a little buttery water) and the kohlrabi, dish with the veal and serve.

My special steak tartare and chips

There is an art to making a steak tartare. It is one of the great skills of 'l'art de la table', as practised by top front-of-house staff. My maître d', Jean-Claude Breton, is truly a master of this art! He will tell you that the main requirement is the very best lean fillet steak from the very best beef, which can only be from well-hung Aberdeen Angus cattle. If you don't have a decent butcher near you, then try one of the excellent family farms now supplying meat by overnight couriers. The next secret of success is to chop the meat by hand, using two razor-sharp heavy duty cook's knives. Often a good butcher will arrange to have your knives sharpened for you – just check what day his knife grinder calls. Finally, for the chips you also need good ingredients. We like to use the Desirée potato and fry it in light olive oil, but groundnut oil is also good, as it can be taken to a high temperature and has a fairly neutral flavour, ideal for deep frying. Note that this recipe contains raw beef and raw egg yolk. **SERVES 2 AS A MAIN DISH**

250g best lean Scottish fillet steak
2 teaspoons finely chopped capers
2 teaspoons finely chopped gherkins
2 teaspoons finely chopped red onion
2 teaspoons finely chopped fresh parsley
2 teaspoons tomato ketchup
2 teaspoons Dijon mustard
$\frac{1}{2}$–1 teaspoon crushed sea salt
a few dashes each of hot pepper
  and Worcestershire sauces
1 large free-range egg yolk
  (ideally the best organic)

Chips
400g medium Desirée potatoes, peeled
light olive oil or groundnut oil, for deep frying
sea salt, to sprinkle

1 It is important that everything is kept chilled when making this recipe – the chopping board and mixing bowl especially. Don't overwork the beef, so the texture remains fresh. Cut the beef into thin slices, then cut the slices into very thin strips. Gather a few strips together and cut across in very tiny cubes. (See photographs of this technique on page 220.)
2 Place the beef in the chilled bowl, spreading the meat up the sides of the bowl to chill further. Add all the remaining ingredients and mix quickly together with a fork until well blended. Shape into two patties and place on chilled plates. Cover and set these in the fridge to keep cool whilst you make the chips.
3 Cut the potatoes into 1cm thick sticks. Don't rinse them – simply lay out on a cloth, season with salt and leave to 'dégorge' for 5 minutes, to dry out a little. Pat dry.
4 Heat a 5cm depth of oil in a deep frying pan to 180°C. Slip the potato sticks into the hot oil (ideally in a frying basket) and fry for 3 minutes or so until softened but not browned. Remove from the oil, and reheat it again to 180°C. Return the chips and fry until golden brown and crisp. Drain on kitchen paper towel and sprinkle with salt.
5 Serve the chips in a bowl separate from the steak tartare.

Braised oxtail with parsnip purée

Oxtail is one of the great British country classic dishes. During the beef ban they weren't available, but now the clusters of oxtail cuts are back in good butchers' shops, and we can enjoy the rich, velvety meat that softens in long, slow cooking. The slices step down in size as the tail narrows. Ideally, you need two good slices per portion. You may find it wise to buy two oxtails and have some leftover for the next day, or to freeze. A comforting parsnip mash is great for soaking up the rich gravy-sauce. This one is a reminder of my first restaurant, the Aubergine. Parsnip purée was so popular, I had to keep it on the menu until I got tired of cooking it. Now, I can reintroduce it. Both elements of this dish can be cooked the day ahead and reheated to serve – another plus in its favour. **SERVES 4 AS A MAIN DISH**

2 oxtails, about 1kg each, cut in 3cm slices
400ml red wine
1 sprig fresh thyme
1 bay leaf
4 tablespoons olive oil
2 carrots, chopped
1 red onion, chopped
1 litre Dark Chicken Stock (page 212)
sea salt and freshly ground black pepper

Parsnip purée
4 medium dumpy parsnips
25g butter
1 tablespoon olive oil
1 medium potato, peeled and roughly chopped
300ml Light Chicken Stock (page 212)
150ml double cream

1 Marinate the oxtails in the wine. The easiest way to do this is to pop the oxtail into a large food bag and pour in the wine and herbs. Seal the bag and rub all together. Store in the fridge overnight.

2 When ready to cook, remove the oxtails and reserve the wine. Heat 2 tablespoons of the olive oil in a large cast-iron casserole and brown the oxtail pieces in succession. Drain on kitchen paper towel.

3 Heat the remaining oil in the pan and sauté the carrots and onion for about 5 minutes until softened. Add the wine marinade (with herbs) and cook until reduced by two-thirds. Pour in the stock and bring to the boil. Return the oxtail pieces and season nicely, then cover and simmer on the gentlest of heats for almost 3 hours until the meat is very tender and falls from the bone when prodded.

4 Meanwhile, make the parsnip purée. Peel the parsnips and cut thick 'chips' from around the core. Discard the core. Chop the parsnips roughly. Heat the butter and olive oil in a shallow saucepan and gently sauté the parsnips and potato until pale golden brown. Pour in the stock, season and bring to the boil. Cover with one or two butter papers and simmer for about 15 minutes until the vegetables are soft and the liquid has evaporated.

5 Pour in the cream, bring back to the boil and simmer for a few minutes until almost all gone. Scoop into a food processor and whiz until very velvety and smooth. Check the seasoning.

6 Dish the oxtails onto warmed serving plates or a large serving platter. Strain the cooking liquid, reheat and nappé the oxtail. To garnish, I suggest diagonal slices of carrots cooked with a little butter, water and crushed garlic. Really nice. Serve with the parsnip purée.

Crispy pig's trotters

This recipe is a labour of love, but if you have ever eaten stuffed trotters, and love cooking, then you'll want to try making them. Pig's trotters generally have to be ordered ahead – make sure you get them with a long length of bone, about 15cm, above the actual hoof. You can order the gammon knuckles at the same time. A razor-sharp thin-bladed knife is essential, because you need to skin the trotters cleanly. I like to serve this with fried quail's eggs and wafer-thin slices of fresh truffle on top – very posh bacon and eggs. **SERVES 4 AS A MAIN DISH**

2 gammon knuckles, to give you about
   500g meat after cooking
4 long-length pig's trotters, singed of hairs
1 onion, half sliced and half diced
2 carrots, diced
1 stick celery, diced
1 fresh bouquet garni (a bay leaf, sprig
   fresh thyme, crushed parsley stalks
   and celery leaf tied together)
4–5 tablespoons olive oil
4 fat cloves garlic, chopped
1 bay leaf
1 sprig fresh thyme

4 teaspoons tomato purée
1 bottle red wine
1 litre Dark Chicken Stock (page 212)
1 pair sweetbreads, prepared and cooked
   (see Sweetbreads with Shallot and
   Mushroom Marmalade, page 147),
   then cut in 6–8 pieces (optional)
sea salt and freshly ground black pepper

To serve (optional)
mixed salad leaves
Classic Vinaigrette (page 213)

1 Start the preparation 24 hours ahead. First, put the gammon knuckles in separate bowls of cold water and set aside to soak. Then skin the trotters. Using a very sharp, thin-bladed boning knife, score right down the thick skin of one trotter to the top of the first knuckle. Working the knife tip under the skin, start to shave away the skin from the bone. Try to ensure you don't take any fat or veins with the skin. Keep shaving and pulling the skin away until you get right down to the first knuckle.

2 Hold the trotter in a clean cloth and let the skin fall over your hand. Score round the partly exposed knuckle and pull the skin away. You should now be able to cut away the long bone, leaving you with a large, loose flap of skin and the end of the knuckle with the toes still attached. It should look like an empty glove puppet at this point. One final tip is to try not to nick the skin as you work it from the bone – I know it might be difficult, but it will stop the filling spilling out later on.

3 Skin the other trotters the same way. To encourage you in this labour of love, let me tell you that my young chefs can skin a trotter in 12 seconds, or so they claim. I've never timed them, but they do work fast and clean.

4 Put the trotter skins in a bowl of cold water and soak for 24 hours to remove any vestiges of blood. Drain and pat dry with kitchen paper towel.

5 When ready to cook, drain the gammon knuckles and put in a pan of fresh water to cover. Add the sliced onion, half the carrots and celery, the bouquet garni and pepper. Bring to the boil, skimming off any scum, and simmer very gently for 2 hours until the liquid reduces right down.

6 Allow to cool, then strain the gammon stock. Shred the meat from the bone and set aside. Discard the vegetables and bouquet garni. Boil the gammon stock down until reduced by half, then set aside. It should set to a jelly as it cools.

7 Sauté the rest of the onion, carrot and celery in 2 tablespoons of the oil for 5–10 minutes until softened and caramelised. Add the garlic, bay leaf, thyme and tomato purée and cook for 2 minutes, then pour in all the wine. Cook right down until reduced by three-quarters.

8 Pour in the chicken stock and add the trotter skins. Bring to the boil, then partially cover and simmer very gently for 3½–4 hours. Do not stir the trotters if you can help it, as you might cut the skin by mistake. The skin is ready when you can press a piece on the side of the pan with your two fingers and pierce it easily. Cool for 10 minutes in the cooking liquid, then carefully remove to a wire rack and cool further. Discard the liquid.

9 Now you can cut off the toes. You should have four large pieces of very soft, deep red trotter skin. Pat them dry. Line a chopping board with a large sheet of cling film. Lay a trotter skin along the length, and fix another skin butting up to the first and slightly overlapping it. Repeat with the other two skins, to make a rectangle of trotter skin some 35–40 x 15cm. Brush generously with the partially set gammon stock. This helps to hold it all together. (In the restaurant kitchen we spread a thin layer of chicken mousseline on the skin, but gammon stock will do almost as well.)

10 Lay the shredded gammon down the centre, mounding it up neatly. If using the sweetbreads, put half the gammon on the trotter skins, arrange the sweetbreads on top, nicely spaced out, and cover with the rest of the gammon.

11 Fold one side of the skin over the filling firmly and neatly, and roll evenly into a 'sausage'. Wrap well in foil, making sure there are no gaps or bubbles, and twist the ends tightly. Chill for 12 hours at least.

12 When you are ready to serve, use a very sharp or serrated knife, dipped in hot water, to slice the roll into 12 medallions. Heat the last of the oil in a frying pan and quickly fry the medallions for about 3 minutes on each side until crispy. Serve the trotters on a well-dressed mixed salad.

Orange and lemon tart

We are frequently complimented on the orange and lemon tart we serve at the restaurant, though I would say that the perfect French lemon – or lemon and orange – tart really depends on the skill of the cook, rolling out the rich sweet pastry until very thin without it breaking, boiling the fruit juices to concentrate the flavour and then baking the filling at a very low temperature until it is just softly set. As a final flourish, we add the thinnest crisp sugar crust, made not just with one caramelised sugar dusting, but two. Try it. **SERVES 4–6**

1 quantity rich sweet pastry (see Pear and Frangipane Flan, page 153)
2 tablespoons icing sugar
Confit of Orange and Lemon (page 215), optional

Filling
600ml orange juice
juice of 2 lemons
grated zest of 1 lemon
grated zest of 1 orange
180g caster sugar
6 free-range egg yolks, beaten
150ml double cream

1 Roll out the pastry dough as thinly as you are able, to a round about 30cm in diameter, large enough to line a 20cm flan tin, 2.5–3cm deep, comfortably with overhang. You could do this on a lightly floured board, or between two lightly floured sheets of cling film. Lift the dough on the rolling pin into the flan tin (or a flan ring set on a heavy, flat baking sheet). Press the dough well onto the bottom and sides of the tin and pinch together or patch any gaps with dough trimmings. There should be a fair amount of overhang (don't trim it off). Place the tin on a baking sheet.

2 Fit a large sheet of foil into the pastry case, bringing it well up the sides. Fill with baking beans. Chill for 20 minutes, whilst you preheat the oven to 180°C, Gas 4.

3 Bake the pastry case blind for 12–15 minutes until just set. Remove the foil and beans. Return the pastry case to the oven to bake for 5 more minutes. Trim the top of the pastry case level with the tin using a very sharp knife, then set aside to cool whilst you make the filling.

4 Reduce the oven temperature to its lowest setting, ideally 100°C. (Many domestic ovens don't get this low and hover around 120°C.) Allow approximately 20 minutes for the temperature to fall.

5 For the filling, boil the orange and lemon juices together until reduced to about 170ml. Cool. Beat the lemon and orange zest with the sugar and egg yolks. Add the cream and then the cooled juice.

6 Place the pastry case on the pulled-out oven shelf and slowly pour in the filling, taking it up to as near the rim of the case as possible. Very, very carefully push the tart back into the oven and bake for about 35 minutes. The filling should still be quite soft. Turn off the oven and leave the

tart to cool inside until it sets enough so that it can be removed without spilling. Cool completely until lightly set, then chill.

7 Sift half of the icing sugar over the top of the tart in an even layer. Immediately caramelise the sugar with a blow torch. Let this cool and crisp, then sift another layer of icing sugar on top and caramelise that. Leave to cool completely.

8 Cut the tart into portions using a long sharp knife and serve with a trickle of cream if you like. We also add a decoration of confit of orange and lemon slices. Should the mood arise, then do try to make them as they are a nice complement to the tart.

Apple, prune and butterscotch compote

*My desserts are always served in diminutive portions. I reckon after four or five courses,
my guests want just a taster or two of an intensely flavoured dessert. This is such a sweet –
delicious Armagnac-soaked Agen prunes served in small shot glasses topped with an apple
and butterscotch purée and thick creamy yogurt. The yogurt can be strained overnight to make
it even more luscious. If you wish to serve larger portions, then spoon into small wine glasses.*

SERVES 4–8, DEPENDING ON SERVING SIZE

100ml Armagnac, Calvados or other brandy
8–10 plump semi-dried (*mi-cuit*) Agen prunes
1 large Granny Smith apple, peeled, cored and chopped
1 vanilla pod
100g caster sugar, plus 2 tablespoons
100g unsalted butter
100ml double cream
about 300g Greek-style whole-milk yogurt

1 Heat the brandy of your choice in a small saucepan, without letting it boil. Remove from
the heat and stir in the prunes. Leave to macerate overnight.
2 The next day, drain the prunes, remove the stones and chop the flesh roughly. Set aside.
3 Put the chopped apple in another small pan, and trickle over 2 tablespoons of water. Slit
the vanilla pod and, using the tip of the knife, scrape out the seeds. Mix with 2 tablespoons
of the sugar, add to the pan and stir into the apple. Heat until sizzling, then cover and cook
for 5–7 minutes, stirring occasionally, until soft and pulpy. Cool, then crush to a chunky purée
with a fork.
4 In another saucepan, gently heat the remaining sugar with a splash of water until melted,
stirring occasionally. When clear, raise the heat, stir in the butter and cook to a light caramel
colour. Do not stir or you will make fudge.
5 Remove from the heat and cool for 5 minutes, then mix in the cream. Cool to room
temperature, then mix in the apple and chill.
6 Divide the prunes among the glasses of your choice. Stir the yogurt until smooth, then
spoon half on top, followed by the apple mixture. Finally, finish with the rest of the yogurt.

Note: I also add tiny sprigs of sugared coriander leaf to decorate. Make these by dipping sprigs
of fresh coriander into beaten egg white and then caster sugar, and leaving to dry on non-stick
baking parchment.

Praline soufflés

Don't think you cannot possibly make a hot sweet soufflé for pudding. We make dozens a day, and all arrive at the table as towering triumphs. It is true that you will have to disappear into the kitchen to whisk the egg whites and fold them into the base mixture. And yes, you will have to wait 15 minutes for the soufflés to cook, but at a private party most people expect to have a good pause after the main course, to truly appreciate the trouble you have gone to for the dessert. Also, it's a good excuse for another glass of wine. **SERVES 6**

250ml creamy milk
100g caster sugar
140g Praline (page 215)
40g plain flour
4 large free-range eggs, 2 of them separated
a little melted butter, for the ramekins
icing sugar, to dust (optional)

1 First make the base mix. Heat the milk with 50g of the caster sugar and 110g of the praline in a heavy-based saucepan.
2 Meanwhile, beat together the flour, 2 whole eggs and 2 yolks in a large bowl. Place the bowl on a damp cloth to hold it steady, and gradually whisk in the hot praline milk. Beat well, then return to the pan and cook on a gentle simmer until very thick and smooth. Remove and cool.
3 Have ready the 2 egg whites and remaining caster sugar. Brush the inside of six ramekins (about 8.5cm diameter) with melted butter and dust with the remaining praline, shaking out any excess. Place on a baking sheet. Preheat the oven to 190°C, Gas 5.
4 When ready to cook, whisk the egg whites until thick and glossy and holding soft peaks. Gradually whisk in the sugar. Fold the meringue (as it is now) into the base mix. Spoon this into the ramekins right up to the rim, and spread the tops level with a palette knife.
5 Bake for 15 minutes until risen and firm. If you have time, sift some icing sugar on the tops, although you may prefer to walk quickly to the table with the soufflés.

Note: Here's a useful tip. Instead of decanting the baked soufflés onto a tray, take the baking sheet straight to the table and scoop off the ramekins with a fish slice onto waiting dessert plates.

My plum tarts

This takes me back to my days as a catering student in Oxford. The idea is based on tarte Tatin, *but uses sliced red plums. The ingredients are simple, but the method needs to be followed carefully. You need tartlet tins (without loose bases) about 10cm diameter, or use Yorkshire pudding tins.* SERVES 4

about 400g rich sweet pastry (see Pear and Frangipane Flan, page 153)
12 large red plums
50g unsalted butter
80g caster sugar
4 whole cloves

1 Roll out the pastry dough to 5mm thickness. Cut out four 12cm rounds, re-rolling if necessary. Prick the centres of the rounds lightly and set aside.
2 Cut the plums in half, remove the stones and slice each half into four. Divide the butter among four tartlet tins and smear over the bottom. Sprinkle 20g of sugar into each tin. Preheat the oven to 190°C, Gas 5.
3 Press the plum slices into the butter and sugar, and press a clove in the centre of the fruit in each tin. Set the tins in a large frying pan and place over a steady heat.
4 The butter and sugar will start to melt and caramelise in the heat. Tilt and roll the frying pan over the heat to shake the tins a bit and even out the browning. After a few minutes you may notice some juice seeping out from the plums. Wrap your fingers in a cloth, then lift up each tin and tip the juice out. This helps to keep the plums dry and caramelise them even more. When the plums look lightly caramelised, remove from the heat and cool slightly.
5 Set a pastry round over each tin and tuck the edges down inside the rim. Prick the tops once or twice, and bake for 12–15 minutes until the pastry is golden brown and crisp. Remove and cool.
6 To serve, fit a dessert plate over each tart tin and carefully upend. Serve with cream, mascarpone or crème fraîche.

Winter fruits in Malibu syrup with mascarpone quenelles

This is a quick hot pudding – sliced winter fruits steeped in a hot syrup laced with Malibu. As a flavour variation, when making the syrup, I caramelise the sugar first until light golden brown, then add the water and simmer for a minute or two. Serve the fruits in shallow fruit dishes and top with quenelles of whipped cream and mascarpone, which melt as you serve. Golden quinces from the Mediterranean can be found in Greek and Lebanese delis during the winter. They are hard, so cut with a sharp knife and keep a firm grip on them. SERVES 4–6

100g caster sugar
1 strip lemon zest
2 tablespoons Malibu or white rum
about 50g fresh cranberries
1 quince
1 large pear
1 large Cox's apple
4 red plums, stoned
1 just ripe banana
40g icing sugar, sifted
Coconut Tuiles (page 215) or shortbreads
  (see Roasted Figs with Cinnamon
  Shortbreads, page 91), to serve

Quenelles
150ml double cream
2 teaspoons caster sugar
1 vanilla pod
3 tablespoons mascarpone, softened

1 Melt the caster sugar with a splash of water in a heavy-based saucepan, stirring once or twice. Raise the heat and, without stirring, cook to a light golden caramel.

2 Remove and plunge the base of the pan into a bowl of ice-cold water to stop the browning. Cool until warm, then stir in 200ml water and the lemon zest. Return to the heat and stir until you have a golden syrup. Boil for a minute or so, then add the Malibu and cranberries, and set aside.

3 Peel and core the quince and pear. Core the apple, but leave the skin on. Slice these fruits thinly along with the plums and banana. Put all the fruits in a bowl.

4 Heat a large non-stick frying pan until very hot. Sprinkle the icing sugar over the fruits and toss to coat, then immediately tip them all into the dry hot pan. Shake the pan well and carefully turn the fruits, which by now should be caramelising nicely. Cook for a minute or so, then mix with the cranberry and Malibu syrup. Cool until just warm. Remove the lemon zest strip.

5 For the quenelles, whip the cream with the sugar until softly stiff. Slit the vanilla pod and scrape out the seeds with a knife tip. Mix the seeds into the cream along with the softened mascarpone. Chill lightly.

6 When ready to serve, divide the fruits among sundae dishes or shallow bowls. Using two dessertspoons dipped in hot water, shape the cream into 4–6 quenelles and place on top of the fruits. Serve with coconut tuiles or shortbreads.

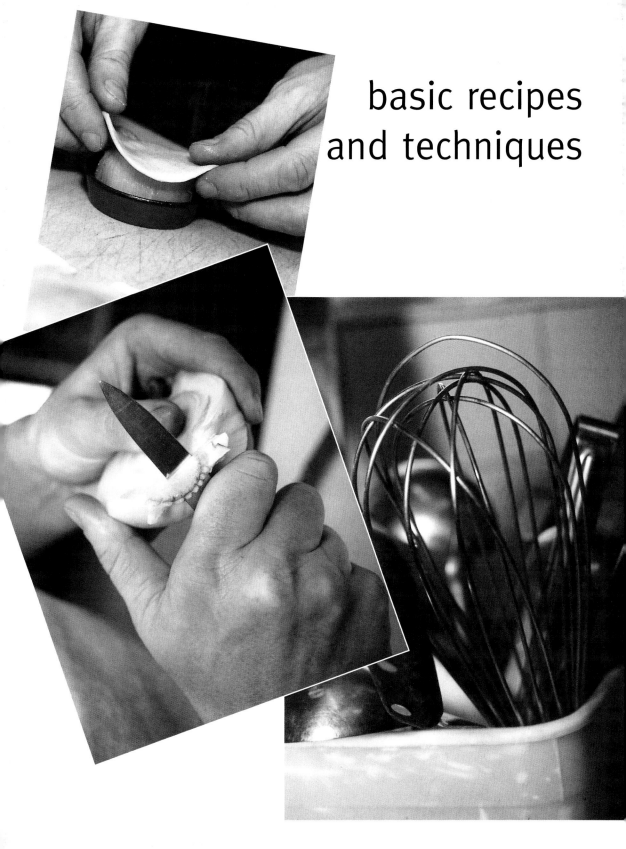

basic recipes and techniques

Several of my recipes require standard preparations, which in a restaurant kitchen we always have to hand. For those that can be kept, I suggest you make up good-size batches and either store in the fridge or freezer. The stocks are most useful frozen in 200ml and 500ml blocks. (Do label them before freezing – they can all look the same once frozen!)

The stocks are best strained through muslin, which can be easily bought from haberdashers or good kitchen equipment stores. It is very cheap and can be washed in the machine time and time again. Failing that, a large J-Cloth is just as good.

Light chicken stock

Place 3kg raw chicken carcasses or bony joints in a large stockpot. Add a good 5 litres of cold water, 3 quartered onions, 2 chopped leeks, 2 large chopped carrots, 4 chopped celery sticks, 1 small head garlic (cut in half widthways), 1 large sprig fresh thyme and 1 tablespoon sea salt. Bring slowly to the boil, skimming off any scum that rises using a large metal spoon (not slotted because the scum can drain through). Boil for 5 minutes, then turn the heat right down and simmer for 3–4 hours. Cool and allow the solids to settle. Line a colander with a sheet of wet muslin and slowly pour the stock through. Cool and chill. This can be kept in the fridge for up to 3 days or frozen. It makes about 3 litres of lovely stock.

For **dark chicken stock**, first roast the chicken carcasses in a preheated 200°C, Gas 6 oven for about 20 minutes, turning frequently. Drain off the fat and proceed as above.

Vegetable nage

One of the most useful stocks to have on hand, this is made slightly differently from other stocks.

Put the following ingredients into a large stockpot: 3 chopped onions, 6 chopped carrots, 2 chopped celery sticks, 1 chopped leek, 1 small head garlic (split in two widthways), 1 quartered lemon, ¼ teaspoon each white and pink peppercorns, 1 small bay leaf and 4 star anise. Pour in 2 litres of cold water, bring slowly to the boil and simmer for 10 minutes. Remove from the heat and mix in 200ml dry white wine. Add a sprig each fresh

tarragon, basil, coriander, thyme and curly-leaf parsley. Cool, then decant into a large bowl and store in the fridge for a good 24 hours. Strain through a muslin-lined colander. This can be kept in the fridge for up to 4 days or frozen. Makes about 1.5 litres.

Fish stock

White fish bones are the most useful, e.g. those from turbot, sole, haddock, hake and so on, not oily fish such as salmon. You'll need about 1.5–2kg of bones. If using fish heads too, cut out the eyes and the gills.

Gently sweat 1 small chopped onion, 1 chopped leek, 1 chopped celery stick, 1 small chopped bulb fennel and 2 whole garlic cloves in a little olive oil for 10 minutes. Add the fish bones (and heads) and 300ml dry white wine, and cook until the wine evaporates. Cover with about 3 litres of cold water, and add a fresh bouquet garni (bay leaf, sprig fresh thyme and some parsley stalks tied together), 1 small sliced lemon and a few white peppercorns. Bring to the boil, skimming well, then simmer for 20 minutes only – no longer or the stock will become bitter. Cool so the solids settle, then strain through a muslin-lined colander. This can be kept for up to 3 days in the fridge or frozen. Makes 2.5 litres.

Court bouillon

Use this for poaching lobsters and whole fish. It can be used up to three times, straining in between.

Simply put all of the following ingredients into a large stockpot: 2 chopped leeks, 3 chopped carrots, 3 chopped onions, 2 chopped celery sticks, 2 chopped bulbs fennel and 4 large garlic cloves (unpeeled). Cover with about 3 litres of cold water and add 1 large sprig each fresh thyme, parsley, basil and tarragon, plus 1 tablespoon sea salt, 2 sliced lemons, 4 star anise and 300ml dry white wine. Bring to the boil, then simmer gently for 30 minutes. Strain through a muslin-lined colander. This can be kept for up to 5 days in the fridge or frozen. Makes about 1.5 litres.

Classic vinaigrette

This has many uses apart from dressing salads.

Whisk together 200ml extra virgin olive oil and 200ml groundnut oil with 1 teaspoon fine sea salt, $1/4$ teaspoon ground black pepper, the juice of 1 lemon, 50ml white wine vinegar and 50ml sherry vinegar. Store in a large screw-topped jar and shake to re-emulsify before use. Makes about 500ml.

Mayonnaise

Whisk 2 free-range egg yolks, 1 teaspoon white wine vinegar, 1 teaspoon English mustard powder and a little seasoning together in a bowl. (Sit the bowl on a damp cloth to hold it steady.) Using 300ml groundnut oil or half groundnut and half light olive oil, drop in a trickle from a teaspoon and beat hard until mixed. Repeat again and again, gradually adding a tad more oil each time, but always make sure the previous amount is well mixed in before adding more. Gradually increase the amount of oil added as the mixture gets thicker and more creamy. When all the oil is mixed in, whisk in 2 tablespoons

cold water. Check the seasoning. This can be kept, stored in a sealed container, for a good week in the fridge. Makes 300ml.

Peach chutney

If you can, use white-fleshed peaches for this chutney. Failing that, yellow peaches will suffice. Buy half of the fruits slightly underripe and a little firm, and the rest slightly overripe and full of flavour. The chutney is also good made with pears, apricots and even mango.

Wash and stone 1kg fresh peaches, then chop into small bite-size pieces. (If using a mixture of slightly underripe peaches and fully ripe ones, set the fully ripe ones aside to add later.) Put the peaches into a large saucepan or preserving pan and add 1 medium cooking apple (peeled, cored and finely chopped), 250g tomatoes (skinned and chopped), 1 finely chopped medium onion, 2 crushed fat cloves garlic, 2 tablespoons grated fresh root ginger, the grated zest and juice of 2 limes, 300g sugar, 1 tablespoon sea salt, 1 teaspoon ground cinnamon, $1^1/2$ teaspoons freshly grated nutmeg, $1^1/2$ teaspoons ground white pepper, 300ml white wine vinegar and 125g flaked almonds. Bring slowly to the boil, stirring until all the sugar has dissolved. Simmer, uncovered, for about 15 minutes, stirring once or twice. Add the ripe peaches (if using), return to a simmer and continue cooking for a further 10 minutes. The mixture should be nice and syrupy, with the underripe peaches still holding a little texture.

Whilst the chutney is bubbling merrily, wash and dry two jam jars

(about 450g size) and place in a warm oven so the jars get hot and are sterilised. Fill the chutney into the jars, place waxed pot-discs on top and screw on the lids. Leave until cold, then label and store. The chutney will keep well, unopened, for a good few months, but once opened, store it in the fridge. Makes about 1kg.

Confit of ceps

Wash 400g fresh ceps and dry well with kitchen paper towel. Remove the stalks and dice. Dice the caps too. Heat 2 tablespoons olive oil in a large frying pan and quickly sauté the ceps until lightly browned. Remove from the heat. Heat 200g goose fat to the lowest temperature your hob can go, preferably below 100°C. Add 1 sprig fresh thyme and stir in the ceps. Cook very gently for about 15 minutes, then cool in the fat. Transfer to a clean jar and store in the fridge until required.

Pickled girolles

You can store these in a jar in the fridge and use them in many different ways, just as you would capers or chunky relishes.

Trim the bases of about 300g small winter girolles. Wash to remove any dirt, then pat dry with kitchen paper towel. Make up 300ml Classic Vinaigrette (see left) and bring to the boil in a saucepan. When boiling, stir in the girolles. Return to the boil, then remove from the heat and leave to steep until cool. Store in a glass container in the fridge and use within 10 days.

Stock syrup

I flavour my stock syrups in various ways – you may find a strip or two of lemon zest is best for general uses, but other ingredients could include a cinnamon stick, split stalk of lemon grass or even a couple of star anise.

Slowly dissolve 250g caster sugar in 500ml water. When clear, add the flavouring and simmer for 5 minutes, then cool. The stock syrup will keep for a good month in the fridge; thereafter it benefits from re-boiling. Makes 700ml.

Puff pastry

Bought puff pastry may be convenient and good at rising evenly, but nothing beats home-made for buttery flavour and melt-in-the-mouth texture. Make this in a large batch and freeze in easy-to-use blocks.

Divide 500g chilled butter into 450g and 50g. Do the same with 500g of plain flour sifted with ¼ teaspoon salt. Cut the 450g of butter into small dice and mix with the 50g flour (do this in a food processor if possible). Spoon onto a large sheet of cling film and shape into a large rectangle about 14 x 20cm. Try to keep the edges neat, as it helps later on. Set aside.

Rub the 50g butter into the 450g of flour. (This is best done in a food processor.) Trickle in 1 teaspoon of fresh lemon juice and enough ice-cold water so the mixture just comes together in a mass – this may take up to 300ml of water, added gradually. Knead lightly to a smooth dough. Roll out on a lightly floured board to a rectangle about 25 x 35cm, keeping the edges neat and straight with even corners. Place the butter rectangle on one side and fold over the other half of the dough to enclose it. Press the edges to seal.

Carefully roll out the dough until it is about three times as long as it is wide. Make sure the butter doesn't break through. Now, fold the top third down and fold the bottom third over it, like a blanket. Give the dough a quarter turn and roll out again, dusting lightly with flour as necessary. Fold again into three, and wrap in cling film. Chill to rest for 20 minutes, then repeat the rolling and folding twice more. Try to remember to do the folding and turning in the same direction. Divide the pastry dough into two or three portions as required and wrap in cling film. Use some and freeze some. Makes 1.2kg.

Crème anglaise

If you have never made a rich custard before, you might want to have a large bowl of iced water at the ready, so you can plunge the base of the pan into it to cool it quickly. Another useful hint is that you can use a sugar thermometer or instant-read thermometer to check if the custard is cooked enough – the temperature should be 82°C.

Slit a vanilla pod in half and scoop out the seeds on the tip of the knife. Put 250ml each milk and double cream in a heavy-based saucepan and mix in the vanilla seeds. Add the pod too. Heat until the liquid starts to rise up in the pan, then remove from the heat and allow to infuse for 10 minutes. Meanwhile, put 6 free-range egg yolks and 90g caster sugar in a large bowl set on a damp cloth (to hold it steady) and beat with a balloon whisk until pale golden and creamy. Remove the vanilla pod from the infused milk, then bring back to the boil. Tip in small slurps onto the sugar and yolks, whisking hard. When the mixture is well blended, return it to the pan on the lowest heat possible. Stir with a wooden spoon for about 2 minutes until the mixture starts to thicken and just coats the back of the spoon. Do not overheat or it will curdle. Strain, cover and leave to cool, stirring occasionally to prevent a skin from forming. Makes 600ml.

Thyme icecream

Heat 250ml creamy milk and 250ml double cream in a large saucepan until the liquid starts to creep up the sides of the pan. Stir in the leaves and flowers from 3 sprigs fresh thyme and leave to get cold.

Put 6 free-range egg yolks and 90g caster sugar in a large bowl, placed on a damp cloth to hold it steady. Using a hand-held electric mixer, whisk the mixture until it becomes thick and creamy. Reheat the milk and cream mixture and, when the liquid rises up again, pour into the yolk mixture whilst whisking with the mixer running on slow. Whisk until well blended. Strain the liquid back into the pan through a sieve (discard the thyme). On the lowest heat possible, stir with a wooden spoon until the mixture thickens and coats the back of the spoon. Don't let it overheat or it will surely curdle and become grainy. Cool the custard, stirring occasionally to stop a skin from forming. (Ideally, cool quickly by standing the pan in iced water.) Churn in an electric icecream machine until the mixture becomes a thick, swirly slush. Scoop into a plastic freezer container and freeze for a few hours, then scoop into shapes to serve. We use two teaspoons to make quenelles, but you may find a ball-shape scoop easier. Serves 4.

Fromage blanc sorbet

Tangy and pure white, this is a very refreshing palate cleanser or light accompaniment to buttery sweet puds. It is best made in an electric icecream machine that will churn it to a creamy texture. The peppercorns add an intriguing spicy hint.

Bring 350ml Stock Syrup (page 214) to the boil with 4 black peppercorns, then cool and chill. Remove the peppercorns and mix in the juice of 1 lemon. Beat into 400g 8%-fat fromage frais using a balloon whisk, then churn in an electric icecream machine until creamy. Scoop into a freezer container and freeze until firm. Serve in scoops or quenelles, or, for shavings, scrape with a metal spoon. Serves 6.

Lemon sorbet

Bring 600ml water to the boil. Stir in 250g caster sugar until it dissolves, then return to a good simmer and cook for 5 minutes. Remove from the heat and stir in the the grated zest of 1 lemon and the juice of 3 lemons. Cool, then strain and chill. Churn in an icecream machine to a soft, icy texture, then scoop into a freezer container and freeze. About 10 minutes before serving, remove from the freezer and soften at room temperature. Serves 6.

Coconut tuiles

One of our popular biscuits, we serve these with all manner of desserts.

We make them small and dainty, but you may prefer a more generous size.

Grind 40g desiccated coconut as finely as possible in a food processor. Add 40g icing sugar and 15g plain flour and whiz again to mix. Pour in 1 beaten free-range egg white and 1 tablespoon melted butter, and process to a thick runny paste. Preheat the oven to 180ºC, Gas 4. Drop 4–6 teaspoonfuls of the coconut mixture onto a baking sheet lined with non-stick baking parchment or a silicone cooking liner. Using a small palette knife dipped in cold water, spread out the mixture evenly and thinly to small rounds. Bake for about 7 minutes until firm, but not coloured. Remove from the oven, wait a minute or so, then lift onto a wire rack to cool and crisp. Repeat with the rest of the mixture. If the biscuits harden before you can lift them off the baking sheet, simply return to the oven to soften for a few seconds. If you want curved roof-tile shapes (tuiles), then drape the warm biscuits over a rolling pin and leave to cool. Makes 12 (or 24 very dainty biscuits).

Confit of orange and lemon

Heat 200ml Stock Syrup (page 214) to boiling. Meanwhile, slice 1 large seedless orange and 1 lemon evenly into 3mm discs, with the peel. Drop the fruit slices into the boiling syrup, then remove from the heat and allow to cool. Remove the confit slices as required; they can be kept in the fridge for up to a month in a covered container. When all the confit slices are gone, you can re-boil the syrup (it will be orange- and lemon-scented) and use again.

Praline

Preheat the oven to 180ºC, Gas 4. Warm 120g flaked almonds in the oven for 10 minutes. Meanwhile, melt 160g caster sugar in a saucepan with a splash of water until clear, stirring once or twice. Add a squeeze of lemon juice, then raise the heat and cook to a light caramel colour. Stir in the almonds, then pour onto a flat baking tray lined with non-stick baking parchment. Leave until cool and set. Crush with a rolling pin into chunks, then grind to very fine crumbs in a food processor. Store in a screw-topped jar and use as required – praline is a delicious topping for an icecream sundae. Makes 280g.

Preparing globe artichokes

We only use the 'heart' of the globe artichoke, which is the meaty base enclosed in tough leaves and protected by a spiky 'choke' in the centre.

Once you have cut off the artichoke stalk (1), peel off the tough outer leaves with your fingers (2). Then, using a small sharp knife, peel round the base of the artichoke to remove all the remaining leaves (3). Trim off the cream- and purple-coloured inner fleshy leaves, cutting straight across just above the meaty heart (4). Turn the heart on its side and, with a larger cook's knife, make a straight cut downwards to trim off the fine fibres of the choke (5). Finally, using the tip of a firm teaspoon, scoop out the base of the fibrous choke (6) to leave just the heart itself. This can be cut into wedges or into thick slices (7), which can then be cut into lozenges.

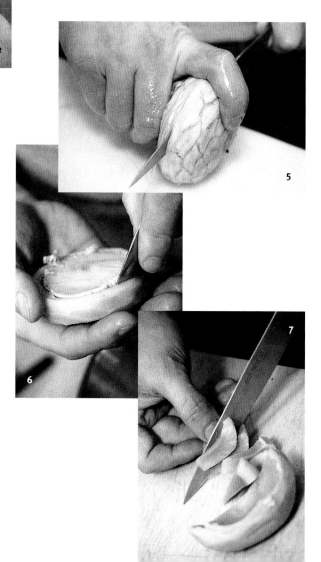

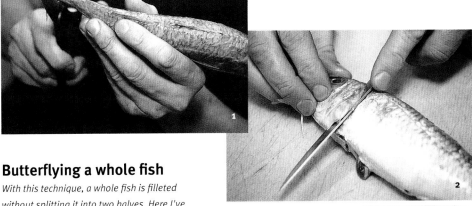

Butterflying a whole fish

With this technique, a whole fish is filleted without splitting it into two halves. Here I've butterflied a red mullet (which is used in the recipe for Baby Red Mullets with Choucroute and Rhubarb on page 184), but any small fish can be prepared in the same way. A very sharp filleting knife with a thin flexible blade is vital, so you can make clean cuts without nicking the skin of the fish.

First, scale the fish, if the fishmonger hasn't done this for you. A red mullet has soft scales, which can be pulled off with fingers (we do this holding the fish inside a bin bag so the scales don't fly everywhere.) Then trim the tail and main body fins with kitchen scissors (1). Cut off the head just above the gills and discard (2). Slit down the belly and pull out the innards, then rinse the fish well in cold running water, running your index finger along the blood line to make sure it is all washed away. Starting on one side of the fish and using the tip of the filleting knife, gently cut the bones away from the flesh – make shaving movements against the bones whilst pulling the eased flesh away with your other hand (3). Work your way back into the main body of the fish, stopping when you get to the top of the fish and the backbone. You must not cut the skin. Repeat this on the other side, working the 'skeleton' free. When finished, the skeleton will still be attached to the tail. Snip the skeleton away with scissors (4), but leave the tail attached to the filleted fish. Finally, trim the edges of the butterflied fish to remove fine pin bones (5), and run the tips of your fingers across the flesh to check there are no more bones left.

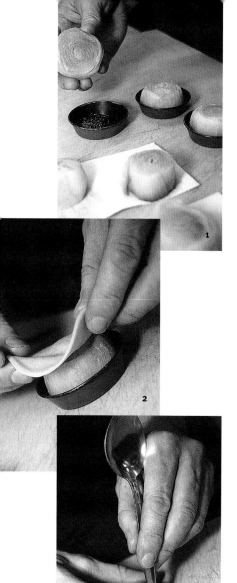

Making chicory tarts

These pretty little tarts, used in the recipe for Gressingham Duck with Chicory Tarts on page 190, are a savoury version of tarte Tatin. There are three elements – a balsamic-flavoured caramel, the base of a chicory head and a disc of puff pastry.

Make the caramel and pour it into the tins. Trim each chicory head so you are left with a dumpy base about 3cm tall. (The tips can be used in salads). Place a chicory base, widest side down, in each tin so it is nicely submerged in the caramel (1). Set a pastry disc on top (2) and tuck it neatly around the chicory using the end of a small spoon (3). After baking, turn out the tarts onto a plate. To enhance the attractive rose effect, separate the chicory leaves slightly with the spoon handle (4).

Shaving sweetcorn kernels off a cob

Very fresh sweetcorn kernels are deliciously tender and juicy. When sweetcorn is in season, I like to shave the kernels off the cob to use in a dish such as Sweetcorn and Spring Onion Risotto (page 68). The kernels also make mighty fine nibbling if you are a little peckish – they're lower in fat than peanuts!

After stripping off the green leaves and silky golden strands, cut off the pointed end of the cob. Stand the cob on end on a wooden board, cut end down and slightly at an angle. Hold the cob firmly by the stalk. Using a sharp cook's knife, cut straight down the cob to remove the kernels in a line. They will probably fly everywhere, so work slowly and carefully. After each cut, turn the cob slightly. Repeat until all the sweet juicy kernels are freed. (The spent cobs can be used in a vegetable nage.)

Making fennel fans

Lots of trimming, peeling and slashing are needed for this, but the technique is actually quite simple, and the end result is very attractive. I serve these in a dish of Red Mullet with Orange-glazed Fennel and Pesto Dressing (page 136).

First, trim off the stalks and feathery fronds (1) – you can use these in other dishes or the fronds as garnish. The outer segments of fennel benefit from a light peeling to make them more tender, so shave off the tough outer ribs with a small sharp paring knife (2). Place the shaved and trimmed fennel bulb upright on a board and cut firmly in half (3). Using the small knife, cut out the base core from each half in a neat 'V' shape (4), but keep the root end intact so the layers of the fennel half still hold together. After braising in buttery stock until tender, transfer the fennel halves to a board, placing them cut side down. With the tip of a cook's knife, slash each half evenly (5), leaving the root end uncut to hold the 'fan' together. Lift the fennel halves onto warmed plates with a palette knife and gently press the slashed flesh to separate and open up the fan (6).

5

6

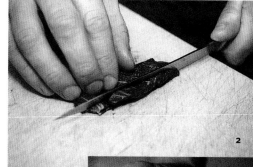

Making gnocchi

Potato gnocchi are fun and easy to make, and are delicious with a warm salad of peas and fèves *(page 24) or rabbit slow-cooked in goose fat (page 145). The potatoes should be quite dry, so either bake them or dry them out in the oven after boiling.*

Mix the mashed potato with flour, egg and the other ingredients to a firm but still soft dough, then divide into balls the size of a small apple. On a lightly floured board, roll out each ball to a cigar shape about 25cm long (1). Flatten the cigar slightly to an oval shape. Using either the back of a table knife or a blunt cook's knife, cut across in 3cm lengths, cutting slightly on the diagonal (2). This will give the gnocchi their characteristic pinched edges. Cook the gnocchi as soon as they have been cut, so they don't dry out.

Making steak tartare

For a perfectly made steak tartare you must have the finest quality free-range, well-hung beef. Mine is Scottish, of course, the very best on the market. The meat must be chopped just once so it retains a clean texture and taste – aggressive chopping and, even worse, mincing, which mangles up the flesh, will destroy the eating quality of the beef and make it taste 'cooked'. My recipe for steak tartare is on page 197.

First, trim any vestige of fat from the fillet, then cut into thin slices (1). Cut each slice into thin strips (2). Gather a few strips together and cut them crossways into tiny, tiny cubes (3). Transfer the finely chopped beef to a metal bowl set in a larger bowl containing iced water (4) so that it will be chilled quickly. Finish by mixing in the flavouring ingredients and then shaping into patties.

1

2

3

4

Making towers

This is a very simple presentation technique that gives an attractive professional finish. It can be used for all sorts of dishes, from creamy risottos and creamed root purées to layers of vegetables topped with fish fillets or neat pieces of meat. Here I'm layering the crab cocktail for the Pepper and Tomato Soup on page 64. You need a deep, straight-sided metal ring such as a plain scone cutter.

Set the cutter in the middle of the plate or soup bowl and spoon in the first layer – here crushed avocado (1). Spread this smooth with the back of the spoon (2). Then add the next layer, which is crab salad (3), and press it down gently (4). Finish with a float of cocktail sauce. Hold your breath and ease the cutter up and away (5). Wipe it clean and start with the next plate.

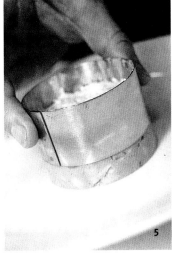

5

Index